CURVES IN CULTURE

Also by Vera Dragilyova

IDEASTHESIA

THE AHA MOMENTS

THE BEST OF ALL WORLDS

UNIVERSAL LANGUAGE BASE

LIFE AS ART

CURVES IN CULTURE

How Social Processes Follow Physical Laws

Vera Dragilyova

Verarta Books

CONTENTS

Introduction

Part 1:   **Definitely, the Beginning   09**

Part 2:   **Social Geometry: Curves   09**

Curve as a social pattern   23
Studying   28
Working   30
Thinking   33
Honesty   35
Power   40
Knowledge   42
Technology   44
Competition   44
Speeding   46
Sense of urgency at work   48
Money   49
Fighting in a relationship   50
Conversation dynamics
Beauty   87
Music   87
Website architecture and discoverability   87
Information   87
Complaining and other negativity curves   53

Part 3:   **Chocolate Hills and Clusters 09**

Similar businesses cluster together 23
Migration to the city 28
What about the food in the boonies? 30

Part 4:   **Categories as Magnets 09**

Immune system: weak vs strong 23
Air conditioners: cold vs mild climate 28
Home heating: hot vs mild climate 30
Climate zones: dry vs rainy 98
Friends vs enemies 90
Rich vs poor 56
Interviews: right vs wrong candidate 56
Culture: insider vs outsider 09
Personality: superior vs inferior 09
Changing lanes: slow vs fast 09
Showing off: rich vs poor 09
Humor: jokes vs insults 09
Relationships: friends vs lovers 09
Texts: serious vs facetious 09
Appreciation: nice vs nasty 09
Fashion: conservative vs rebellious 09
Hair color: platinum blond vs white 09
The uncanny valley: film vs animation 09
Reality: magic realism vs surrealism 09
Offenders: slight vs extreme 09

Products: Italian fashion vs comfort food   09
            Ratings: cheap vs expensive 09
            Envy: amateur vs professional   09

Part 5:   **Pleasure, redefined   09**

            Pleasure as a guideline for living   98
            Sources of pleasure   09
            Types of pleasure   09
            Pleasure and drugs   09
            Physical counterparts of pleasure   09
            A few pleasure opposites   09
            The culture of alcohol   09

Part 6:   **The Game Instinct   09**

            Anatomy of a game   09
                        Azart   09
                        Goals   09
                        Rules   09
                        Challenge   09
                        Response   09
                        Feedback   00
            Examples of games: 09
                        Body   09
                        Family   09

Social communities   09
Social mobility   09
Work   09
Relationships   09
School   09
Politics   09
Art   09
Hobbies   09
Sports   09
Gambling   09
Business   09
Wars   09
Arts and fashion   09
Story structure   09

Part 7:   **Geometry of compassion   09**

Sources of disagreement   09
          Radius of vision   09
          Frames of reference   09
          Anchoring one's perception   09
          Conflicting attributes   09
          Ends vs means   09
          We don't like other opinions 09
Reciprocation   09
          Resistance   09
          Zero sum, or an eye for an eye   09

Part 8:   **Glitches in human nature   09**

Misplaced affection   09
Misplaced aggression   09
Misjudging someone's guilt   09
Inability to recognize false love   09
Believing those who act upset   09
Believing those who act confident   09
Favoring people with good looks   09
Attributing stupidity to kindness   09
Respecting only the respected   09

Part 9:   **Possibly, the end   09**

INTRODUCTION

This book is a sequel to "Ideasthesia", where author explores her mental imagery as part of Synesthesia and Ideasthesia. Synesthesia is a neuropsychological phenomenon, where input into one sense is accompanied by sensations in one or more other senses: for example—seeing sounds, or tasting and hearing colors. Ideasthesia is when abstract ideas are experienced as physical objects and actions in the mind's eye.

Ideasthesia allows humans to experience reality in intense, phantasmagorical ways, producing mental imagery that doesn't simply entertain, but also models hypothetical reality, leading to the most surprising of discoveries. The author is both a Synesthete and an Ideasthete.

That all humans process abstract thoughts in physical terms is a premise in both "Curves in Culture" and "Ideasthesia", with an understanding that it is only a question of awareness that differentiates us. In this book, the author observes that social processes seem to be governed by the laws of physics and chemistry, without trying to prove or disprove anything. A tacit question is whether it is because her mental imagery is physical by nature that she sees social reality this way, or it is because it is really so?

The idea that social processes follow physical laws is so vast and comprehensive that to do it justice would be well beyond the scope of this book. This text is not everything there is to say about this radial view, but only an invitation to ponder, or a seed of an idea really, and a call that awaits a response in the minds of the readers.

Please read this book for the sake of your curiosity, with suspended judgment, inflated sense of humor, and in search of mental pleasure. If this book finds a corner in you where its ideas resonate, and where some intellectual excitement takes place, then its goal has been reached.

Let's dig together into these mental boonies, and make it interesting. Readers are co-creators, after all!

DEFINITELY, THE BEGINNING.

A pendulum is a sign of life.
—Meema Iselfanday

Walking through a busy city crowd is an uphill battle: we are all rushing for our fool's gold, which secretly resides inside us, but we keep thinking that it's elsewhere. A cold shoulder brushed against me, and I would have let go, if not for those familiar piercing eyes I had not seen for years, and a ray of hope that suddenly lit up my whole being.

"Hey you!"—I called out.

"Me?"

"Yes, you, Elsa. No, don't look back, there is no one there."

"What do you want?"—asked Elsa, her body half-turned away from me, her eyes squinting.

"Why did you flake on me the last time?"

"So? I only taught you a lesson: don't tell me everything you know, but only what I don't."

"This time around, it is something you couldn't possibly think to know."

"Sounds suspiciously intriguing, but hopelessly childish,"—Elsa turned her body to me, which clearly meant, she was giving me a chance.

"You are something else, Elsa. Will you ever change?"

"I could become anything—that's the power of imagination, Vera."

"That depends on who is imagining!"

"This time, you are in control."

"Then, let me tell you: I have come up with some perfect little tools for understanding what's going on with people!"

"Not again!"

"This time it's different. This time, it's about how social processes follow physical laws."

"Easy, easy now! I barely made it alive last time!"

"All you have to do is listen and imagine, Elsa, and it will all make sense, especially because you read my first book."

"Ah, yes, the book you never wrote!"

"Thanks to you!"

"What if I daydream from time to time?"

"Oh, knock yourself out. Just sit down here, we have all day."

"Your day is my year, remember? Fine, just speed-talk, and I will keep quiet."

"I will only plant some ideas. Nothing more,"—I covered my mouth with the palm of my hand. Then, I pointed to a soft cushy chair across the table from me, and Elsa sat down. "Where did all this come from?"—she whispered, and her jaw opened as wide as that of a feeding shark. It looked as if she just saw herself in the mirror, fifty pounds overweight.

"Another one of those Freudian sessions,"—I laughed to myself, but Elsa did not seem to hear. She sat down and stretched out her body to fit precisely the shape of the chair, then looked into the sky and closed her eyes, smiling. That was the perfect pose, the perfect face I needed to see, to tell my story. For a moment, I felt like I was a photographer, taking photos with my internal organs, for the lack of a camera.

"Elsa, there is a part of you in this book, between the lines."

"You haven't even written it yet!"—whispered Elsa, without moving her lips or disturbing her smile, her eyes still closed.

"But I have seen it all here,"—I pointed to my head, as if she could see me, and as if I was going shoot through my skull with a revolver. "It is all brewed locally, ya' know."

3

How can anyone tell a story to someone who is barely there? How can anyone show a film to someone who is not even looking? In this cold emptiness, in this silence full of fake smiles, a heinous void of answers that keeps ringing in my ears, I do it anyway. Just get it out into this wide, wild and weary world, I say to myself, and I let it hover, forever entangled into the spiral of its quantum existence, trickling into the uncertainty of space and time—maybe for eons—before any single mind will care to understand.

Meanwhile, in my head—its' a party! Things that no one normally sees take shape and come alive. Societies, personalities, traditions, emotions and thoughts all have bodies. They interact with each other in magical ways, showing solutions that are hard to express in words. Pure mental pleasure, worth living for! I couldn't even start telling the whole story, because I would have to show it, and I couldn't even show it, because I am no movie screen. Now, where would you choose to be? Inside my head or out there, in the cold?

Since Elsa is out to lunch, someone turn the page please.

SOCIAL GEOMETRY: CURVES

A circle is an eternal curve.
—Meema Iselfanday

"I think that I have learned more than just one lesson,"—I said to myself.

"You didn't think that, you only thought of thinking it,"—Elsa insisted in response.

"And you must be right or else, Elsa, right?"

"Never mind."

"Never mine me, just mine yourself!"—I said with a smile, knowing that the war was now on.

Elsa opened her eyes so wide that a sundry sailor could have been swollen by them, were he not careful.

"Vera, you mean, data mining?"

"I mean—never mind. It is all in your mind, Elsa, it's all in that old mind of yours."

"It is not all in the mind!   There is a boisterous reality outside, whether you want it, doubt it, deny it, or not."

"Exactly. And you are always trying to mess with it. Stick to imagination, and we will get along. Or better else, just listen, Elsa. Just listen, and be barely there."

Elsa sighed a sigh as deep as Mariana trench, and I wondered why she did not leave then and there. She was probably in way too deep to leave, or too relaxed in her imaginary chair. "She must be getting old,"—I thought to myself. "Getting old is getting deep and lazy."

I stood up, as if I was a trial attorney, about to deliver an important speech to the grand jury.

"So, here are the lessons to myself, Elsa. Most likely, it is not something that you already know. And it is not what you think, and not even something you thought of thinking."

Elsa nodded silently, pursing her lips, as if in learned helplessness, and as if I was holding her a prisoner.

"Yes, like so, nodding, yes, that's a good idea, my dear. And, speak Latin, when it is your turn to speak, would you?"

"As astra per aspera! And Fiat Lux, let it not?"—Elsa muttered and smiled ever-so-slightly, seeing that I saw that she still had it in her. That heinous spirit of hers. I didn't flinch. She was just letting me rule this time: a gesture of condescension, but I took what I could from it. As always.

"You and your Latin! Ok, Elsa, I will speed-talk and keep it simple."

"I highly doubt you are capable, Vera! Nonetheless, I am all ears, flapping. Entertain me."

"You know that I have Synesthesia and Ideasthesia."

"I will not interrupt!"—Elsa pointed a finger at me, with her eyes still closed.

"Then don't! You don't even have to listen, just pretend!"—I rolled my eyes and continued. "Just to remind you, my brain conceptualizes everything abstract in physical terms, making it all a part of my body, in my mind's eye. Whatever pattern I detect, be it how someone's character changes, or how a society evolves—they all are physical actions to me, with corresponding graphs to represent them. And every time, I think to myself, does anybody see what I see?"

"I have my eyes closed, but I definitely see what you see."

"Oh, I see. I like the way you think, Elsa! Anyway, it occurred to me that social processes follow physical laws. But why? Is it only because I conceptualize them in physical terms, or are they really part of the same fundamental

7

design on which all of our reality is based? I don't know. This is all about looking into it and asking why and how.

This time around, I will talk about curves, clusters, and categories. The three C's! But also, I will talk about pleasure and human character, as well as some glitches in nature. This is about pulling the first string that might unravel a whole knot of civilization, woven all around us, and we are so tied into it that we don't even notice.

Curve as a social pattern.

A curve is such a fundamental pattern of life that any type of a phenomenon can be expressed in terms of it. Think Bell curve, a Gaussian curve, or a Standard Distribution Curve. Think—a belle curve! Any good old curve asks a question: what is the most central/essential quality of something? It answers with its middle peak, and its sides represent all the decreasingly less similar instances.

Even emptiness can be expressed in terms of a curve. The question would be, how empty is this something? Completely empty? Then, it belongs in the middle peak. Somewhat empty? Then, it belongs to the side. Almost full of stuff? Then, move it all the way to the side, into the outlier zone. A curve is really a wave, you know that. Every action in our reality seems to be the product of such waves' overlapping. It is all about the match and harmony, and thus we get to listen to the music of the universe.

This is where the law of moderation comes in: not too much, not too little. And why does it work? In nature everything is based on coincidence: for two planets to collide, they must be at the same place, at the same time. The physical matter of which they are made has to be precisely at that single point, and not a little to the left or to the right. On a curve, each planet must be close to the peak, and not be an outlier—otherwise they will merely miss each other. So it is with people meeting each other, relationships working out, political campaigns being successful. Just take any physical or social activity: they all work on this principle of coincidence and match. Imagine two curves overlapping—do their peaks overlap, too? Or only partially? This will tell you how far or close something is from taking place. When you see everything that happens around you in those terms, everything starts making sense. But it is even more interesting than that!

Let me tell you about how the advice about everything being in moderation really does work! In physical terms, we know that adding some water to the fire will make it glow even stronger, but too much water—will kill it. Watering a plant just right will make it grow, but watering it too much—will make it die. There are a million examples like that in the physical world, where just right is in the middle, and both too little or too much is considered bad. Why, just why does it also work so well in the social space?

Let me give you some examples here that we will both recognize:

Studying.

Studying too little will not provide enough knowledge to pass a test. Studying too much will make the brain will shut off from fatigue. Studying just right will keep you in a good shape physically and emotionally, and just with enough knowledge to succeed.

Working.

Why is it that we all talk about work-life balance? Because everything is moderation, everything in moderation. We work too little, and barely anything gets done. We work too much, and we ourselves will be done for. We work just right—and things come out just right. Again, it is the same curve pattern.

Thinking.

To understand something correctly, one must think just enough, not too much, not too little. Thinking too little will not allow to get to the gist of the matter, thinking too much—and we will start seeing things that are not there.

Honesty.

Too little honesty is an outright sin, a socially harmful thing than no one should do. Too much honesty can become an equally harmful act, albeit for a different reason. This is why there is a concept of white lies. We need them, and you will find out precisely why, if you tell someone how ugly their newborn baby is. Knowing when to be honest, when to keep one's mouth shut, and when to squeeze out a lie to avoid hurting people's feelings is truly an art of moderation.

Power.

No power at all feels terrible. A moderate to high amount of power feels great. Could there be too much power? Eventually, if one could become all-powerful, one might feel lonely, in the absence of equal company and challenges that normally make life exciting. In history, having too much power has caused some fanatics to start world disasters, as as fascism during the World War II.

Knowledge.

This one is complicated. Knowing nothing is inconceivable. Knowing close to nothing is debilitating, or it could be bliss. Not knowing how many people are being tortured this very moment, not knowing the day you will die is probably a good thing, especially because there is nothing you can do about it. Knowing just enough is not only knowing the problems that exist, but also what to do about them. Knowing too much is knowing more problems than you can solve. Knowing too much could also be bliss—because now you know what problems exist and what to do about them. Knowing too much would be knowing about every little detail in the universe, to the point that everything becomes predictable and life stops being a wonder. I guess, the overarching curve is debilitation to exhilaration, to melancholy.

Technology.

When humans invented their first tools—they got more powerful. With the increase of technology, where for every unit of technological increase there is an equal increase in human power—we have arrived at the peak of the curve, at the optimum human power, supported by technology. However, when technology surpasses the human need or the human ability to handle it—there is a great risk of its turning against humans—singularity, for example.

Competition.

No competition at all makes people lazy. A little competition can go a long way in creating the excitement that drives up the quality of whatever activity humans are engaged in. Just the right amount of competition produces optimal results. Too much competition wreaks havoc on all! As competition passes its peak, only criminal measures can help winning, and there is barely a crime that a human will not commit in order to win.

Speeding.

For goodness' sake, speeding is a painful thing to talk about! We all know that one could get a ticket for driving too fast, but most of us also know that one could also get it for driving too slowly. So, the solution is driving just right, within the allowed range. Except, some of us do like it on the bad side of the curve!

Sense of urgency at work.

Some managers are advised to create a sense of urgency in their subordinates, so that they will work harder and get more results. It only works when it is not overdone, and done just right. A little energy spices up things. Too much urgency, and the workers get overstressed, exhausted, and no longer able to control their focus and effort, from mere fatigue.

Money.

There is such a thing as having too much money, it turns out! At least, emotionally and psychologically. Virtually everyone has heard of the studies that show a certain monetary threshold, beyond which any increases in income does not bring more happiness. It appears obvious that poverty is undesirable, but extreme wealth also comes with problems, which is also easy to observe. Somewhere in the middle, hovers that golden Gaussian curve peak, at which the amount of money one has is just right for that particular person, in their particular circumstances. Any more than just right—and we start getting new problems, while the happiness value of that money goes down. In fact, there is an ongoing cycle of curves there! What happens is that, as more money ushers new problems, it also places a person in a new monetary bracket, with its own standards, and its own new curve! In this new bracket, the person is now suddenly seen as poor, relative to others in that category, and needs more money to reach the peak, for the total wellbeing to be at its optimum. So, if someone were struggling to buy their first home and did so, one is it a good place. Then, if that same person wins a $100 million in a lottery, the situation changes drastically: this money becomes a headache! How not to lose them is only the first worry. Where to invest it is the second one. The third is dealing with all the people who want to take it away from you, and the list goes on. The whole social environment must change around this person, in order to deal with this new money, and when it does, the curve cycle starts again.

Fighting in a relationship.

No fighting at all could be either a sign of a good relationship, or a false positive. No fighting at all might mean that the partners are holding it all in and are not communicating, and is a sure sign of a future breakup, both according to research and life experience. Because there are a million natural reasons to disagree in life, a little conflict is unavoidable, and is usually a sign of healthy openness in the relationship. Moreover, resolving conflicts actually deepens and strengthens emotional ties between partners. However, too much fighting, when there is more fighting without any resolution—that is also a sign of a future breakup. Too little fighting turns out to be a negative indicator, just like too much fighting does.

Conversation dynamics.

This is about different levels of intelligence between two people who are having a conversation. In this case, continuum is from low intelligence, to moderate intelligence to higher intelligence, relative to the person in point. If the other person is a lot less intelligent, there would not be many arguments, simply because there would not be much to talk about, and so not much to disagree about. If people are of similar level of intelligence, then their conversation is bound to be interesting, laden with potential arguments. If the other person is a lot more intelligent, then there would most likely not be much of a conversation—since this is exactly the reverse of the first scenario mentioned, and now, it is the other speaker that will not find it interesting to engage. Disagreement is at its minimum when the difference in intelligence is the greatest, and at its maximum the difference is minimal. This curve applies equally to all levels of intelligence. There could be an argument made that people would actually agree faster when they are both highly intelligent, because they will be able to understand each other better. That would be a different curve altogether, because it would focus more on the level of intelligence overall, instead of on the difference between the two speakers.

Beauty.

It is surprising, but statistically speaking, people prefer an average face—a face that is an average of all available human features. This finding could be confirmed with a few clicks, or with a quick thought experiment—when considering extremes. Well, let's take lips. If they are so thin that one can barely see them— those probably will not appeal to most people. If the lips are so big that you can barely see the face behind them— that also would be repulsive to most humans. And that goes for every single feature. There is no such a thing as could not be small enough, or could not be big enough, or something else enough. Everything seems to follow the curve pattern of moderation.

Music.

Music, out of all examples, probably has the most flexible peak—the widest range of what could be accepted as optimal, but every genre would have its own. In Western music, the Classical period would tolerate very little cacophony, but no cacophony at all would also mean a single tone and no harmony. Unless it is an exception of a solo instrument, there must be some musical chords present, which in itself constitutes cacophony, if only to a small degree. Too much cacophony, and the music would not belong to the Classical period any longer. Historically, cacophony has been increasingly accepted; however, extreme cacophony, beyond the threshold of discernible separate sounds would cease to be considered music. Other aspects of music, such as speed, follow the same curve. If music is so slow that we cannot even discern its melody—it is not music, after all. If music is so fast that all we hear is white noise—then, it is white noise, and nothing more.

Website architecture and discoverability.

This is not an obvious example of a curve. When the structure of a website is too shallow, where many pieces of information are displayed on one single page, it is very hard to find anything, and the website stops being usable. When the structure is too deep, each item gets its own page, and so to get to item 55, one would have to go through 54 preceding pages, all linked one to another, before arriving at the needed page. That is certainly not usable at all. The secret to a good design is putting enough items on the page to provide maximum information, but without overwhelming the viewer, so that the information becomes hard to discover. This does not only apply to websites, but to any visual display of information.

Information.

Information in general follows the same curve, in any channel which can carry it: visual, auditory, tactile, olfactory, and gustatory, as well as intellectual or emotional. Too little of it is just that—too little. Too much of it, and a human mind is overwhelmed and is unable to process it any longer. If Braille for the blind has the dots too close to each other—they would not be able to read. Make them too far apart—and one would lose track of them. Mix 50 different perfumes together, and you will smell like nothing at all. Too many ingredients in one sauce—and it tastes like everything and like nothing. Try to be liked by everyone—and you will appeal to no one. From a completely different angle, this is a great trick some lawyers use, when the records of their client are subpoenaed: they provide too many documents to review, burying the key information in them. Technically, they work by the book, but in fact—they put the matter on the right side of the curve, where the utility of the information they provide is at the minimum.

Complaining and other negativity curves.

Not complaining at will get you nowhere, since no one will know of your issues. Complain too much, and people get overwhelmed and turned off. Similarly, scolding children a little, or once in a while, will get them to behave. Too much scolding on the regular basis—and children become immune to it. This particular negativity curve is found in many-many places, because people tend to get numb to things that bother them repeatedly. This also goes for advertising, warning, or threatening too much: they all stop working, because they get blocked out. People develop a blind spot to repetitive negativity. If they cannot get numb to it, they develop a Stockholm syndrome, in the case of victims. It could also turn into a case of Peter-cried-wolf, where negative actions are no longer taken seriously, because they have been repeated too much.

When we try to convince someone, the harder we try, the better are our results. However, when we pass a certain threshold, we start getting the opposite result. That is why a good advice to salespeople is not to oversell: meaning, not to sell after the sale has mentally happened. This is also why you don't want to be overzealous about making someone feel guilty. Your initial accusations may produce some guilt effect, but at a certain point, the person will start fighting back, and these accusations will turn against you. It is the same with a wounded animal: a little would might scare the animal away, but a life threat will turn it into a true beast and will cause a fierce counterattack. It is all about knowing the limits.

I wonder what exceptions there might be to this overwhelmingly widespread curve pattern. Well, this is just the beginning of the exploration, but let me tell you a story. We were carpooling once, on a scorchingly hot day. The driver turned on the conditioner full-force, to make it as cold as possible, so that the stream of air would hit our faces like a fire hydrant to calm our burning cheeks. After only a minute, the surface of our skin stared burning again —not from the heat, but from the cold of the conditioner. I asked the driver to turn it down a little, since now it was too cold— and he did. A minute later, I started feeling the heat creeping up on me again. So, of course, I asked the driver to turn on the 'hydrant' again, and give us some cold air. Another minute passed by, and the cold burning sensation became once again unbearable. Surely, I asked the driver to adjust the temperature—yet again. 'Seriously?'—he said angrily. 'I am never carpooling with you again!' Then, another passenger answered him: 'Yes! Seriously! We don't need it too cold or too hot, we need it just right. What about it don't you understand?'"

Elsa frowned, as if she was seeing herself in the place of that imbecile driver.

"An imbecile!"—she cried out loud, as if she read my mind.

"Oh, it is the epic blueprint for human misunderstanding, and I wouldn't call all of humanity loggerheads, I wouldn't. No wonder, education is considered the art of making finer distinctions. If that driver adjusted the temperature in small enough increments, we would probably arrive at the optimal temperature much faster,"—I said with visibly growing confidence that this conversation was going to be fruitful.

"It used to be like walking on eggshells with you, Elsa. But now, I am either floating in the air, or we are on the Moon."

"Why on the Moon?"

"Because the Moon is about 6 times smaller than Earth, and so there, I would be about 6 times lighter."

"There is the perfect weight solution for ya'!"

"Rather, a perfect illusion for a problem I don't have."

"You know what I like about you that keeps me coming back?"

"A little knowledge is dangerous. Too much is too. I don't know if I want to know."

"It's because we can talk forever, and you always have something new to say."

"Elsa! You have no idea what you just got yourself into!"

"Oh, a little knowledge is so dangerous! That's why I am here."

"So, anyway, from curves to clusters,"—I felt Elsa's insult creeping up on me.

"Yes, patterns in nature repeat themselves."

"That's exactly why we need to look at this."

"You have to keep turning the pages for me. Next!"

"Let me tell you a story first."

"Another story?"

"This is a true story."

"You mean, the rest of what you told me was imaginary?"

"As imaginary as you are, Elsa. And you would never know."

"I have been imaginary for so long, I am starting to believe in myself."

"So, I was driving across the United States, from California coast to New York City, without a map or GPS, just following Highway 80, in an old Honda—ancient—really. I was sure it would be easy, must following one single highway—no turns, no exits, just follow the road eastward. Well, did you know that this highway changes names in many areas? When I was close to New York, my car broke down, and I didn't even know where I was—middle of some boonies."

"And?"

"And at that moment, I realized something."

"Which was what?"

"I'll tell you in a minute."

CHOCOLATE HILLS AND CLUSTERS

Do you know why time exists? It's because if you get everything, and all at once, you will just explode.
—Meema Iselfanday

"It's been five minutes, Vera, and you say nothing. Is this some kind of a trap?"

"Yes, it is a trap, I realized that I was trapped in the middle of a valley between two hills."

"And?"

"Not the hills that you are thinking of, and not that kind of a valley."

"How would you know what I am thinking of?"—asked Elsa, and I rolled my eyes.

"I realized that I have been driving through this immense terrain of invisible hills—the whole continent of North America, from coast to coast, was covered with them, and they were passing right in front of my eyes. They looked exactly like the Chocolate Hills of Bohol, in the Philippines—chocolate because they are reminiscent of Hershey's Kisses."

"So, North America looks like chocolate kisses to you?"

"Yes, it does, and so does the rest of the world. Look around!"

"I knew part of us was imaginary, but this?"

"It looks like people always settle in clusters and never spread out evenly. Unless they are Big Foot! You don't really notice it on a big scale, until you physically drive over that vast space, especially if it is a whole continent. Humans don't act like gas particles, spreading evenly in a container, but more like the galaxies in the Universe—in three-dimensional spirals. Each human cluster looks like a Bohol Chocolate Hill, or like a pyramid of Giza in Egypt, if seen from the side. The center toward which each cluster gravitates socially just looks higher to me somehow. They look like mounds, or hives! The outskirts of a cluster are the edges of such a mound. That is a physical representation I have in my mind of humans settlements and social interaction. It appears to me that all of culture is organized according to the laws of gravity that we observe in the galaxies of the Universe, also seen in any cup of coffee—if your stir it fast enough. Culture is not uniform, but consists of spirals, of these tornadoes that suck in its surroundings. It is like humans gravitate toward each other and seek out interaction, which then become greater than the sum of all humans together.

And really, the whole being greater than the sum of its parts in social processes is mirrored in chemistry, where a combination of elements produces a result that is completely different in nature from its starting components. A vivid example is combining baking soda with vinegar: it causes bubbles that are absent in both ingredients. In social processes, one salient pattern that we can observe is clustering—social organization, where a cluster is always greater than a mere sum of its members. Take any organization: a corporation, school, military, a clique of friends, or a family. The key is the interaction between the units that comprise the whole—both in chemistry and in society. In chemistry—it is the physical properties of molecules and elements, and in society—it is the character of people. A Bohol Chocolate Hill in society is what culture is made of, it is civilization, by definition. It is a system whose gravity does not let its energy escape, it is life itself.

Imagine saying hello to someone, and the person does not react. That's your experience of death, really. Imagine three people sitting in one room, each doing their own thing—looking at their phones, maybe: here, there is no system that could act as a unit, there is no interaction, and there is no life, either. Now, imagine those three people start looking at each other and talking. Now, there is gravity between them, even though it is lose. Then again, imagine that those people are planning a bank heist together. In this case, gravity between them is much stronger, and the group is now a system that keeps much of its energy to itself—energy being their interaction and efforts. From death and entropy—all the way to the tightest organization and life.

A pack of wolves can stock and successfully trap its pray, only because they cooperate. A team of humans in the primordial times could attack a mammoth, only because they conspired together. In the modern times, any type of organization relies on the interactions among its members, conserving of energy within their system, so that the system could hold together and function. It is a clearly repeating pattern. And see how we have nothing but these physical terms to describe it? We don't even have words outside our physical interactions with the world to talk about any social processes!"

"Why are those spirals turning?"

"That is what they do in my mind, all on their own. There are other things I have noticed."

"All of that on Highway 80, driving across the US?"—Elsa laughed.

"Yes, exactly! Having one straight road ahead, all the way through, probably did the trick! It is crazy, but beside galaxy spirals, each center of a settlement looks like a pole, to which rubber bands are attached and then stretched to different lengths, to connect to the ground—the outskirts.

Each city has its particular culture, which, like a rubber band, wields peer pressure to its members, tacitly instructing them on how to live and how to act—all the way down to what to eat and what to wear, how to mow one's lawn, what the children should be doing in their spare time, and what types of crimes get punished. Deciding to which culture one belongs makes a huge difference in one's behavior.

Finally, the most fascinating thing I noticed was that the reason that the outskirts are always worse off in all respects than the center is because they are the outskirts in physical space. Whatever good there is in the outskirts—doesn't last and is pulled toward the center, as if by gravity. The best students go to the best schools, which are at the center. The best businesses go to the center—because this is where all the action happens. It is all about gathering to be conveniently located next to each other—to facilitate the interaction. It is because the center is where physical distances to the all other members of a settlement are a the minimum.

This is how a physical space is copied by a social process. People move toward the center of the city, just like tornado particles are sucked into the center. This is also how a physical space determines the flow from outside to the center—a pattern that is universal, all around the planet, and wherever humans or any other social organisms operate. Other options, such as being evenly distributed, or forming circles that are empty on the inside—those patterns just cannot be found in human settlements, unless it is a round table or a village of a few homes, or it is a government project development. There is a reason why urban planning that doesn't follow natural human ways of settling together causes crime, disorganization, and social malaise. Hm-hm.

Similar businesses cluster together.

I find that there are two separate opposing principles that guide the location of similar businesses. One of them pulls them together, and the other one says that they should be far apart. Just like magnets! The one that pulls them together is this: customers are more likely to

31

notice your business, if it is next to the one they are already visiting, and the customer interest is already matching what the business offers. The one that pulls them apart says that, in order to avoid competition, you should be far away from another business that offers the same product or service as you do. It seems that the first principle of 'pull together' works better, and businesses still make more money if they cluster together.

From the point of view of the customer, seeing more choices side by side not only whets their appetite to explore and buy more, but also appears to be a better deal, to drive to one single location and see more choices than to drive around several locations, wasting time and gas. It is like killing as many birds as there are businesses—with one stone. Of course, it will vary with product, but overall, it looks like sharing a location allows combining customer bases, creating shared value. It is like sharing ideas—you don't lose yours, once you tell someone else about it. So, if the starting situation is so that all businesses are equidistant, the first two businesses that cluster together will have a competitive advantage over others, instantly. The bigger the cluster, the farther the customer is willing to travel to get there. Think giant malls: there is a reason they work so well, even though most of them are located at great distances to the center. Clustering pays off, both for businesses and for its customers!

Migration to the city.

A city is born, and it is nice. Please, smile. As the city grows, there comes differentiation, where the center holds all the best of the best, while the suburbs lag behind. As the city keeps growing, the poor slowly move into the center, in search of work, until the center becomes too crowded for what it can sustain, resulting in its being run down and uncomfortable. In a nutshell.

Then, there is a phenomenon of spoiling a barrel of honey with one spoon of tar. As soon as one single outsider —outskirter—moves into the center, the immediate neighbors start moving away, replaced by more of the outsiders, drawn toward the familiar and filling in the gaps left by previous owners, and one can see a patch of deterioration rapidly growing. Only one undesirable outsider can cause a domino effect, destroying the whole original colony. Eventually, most of the city's rich move to the outskirts, right outside the farthest reaches of the poor, and the city starts looking like a black hole with a shiny band around it. It is like a dying star. As the center of the city stagnates in its poverty, eventually, it becomes a great combination of a low-priced piece of real estate and a great location, and gentrification happens—the city's revival. Now, the center of the black hole is filling out with life, and we are getting something like a rainbow circle, with a developed center, a wide band of increasing poverty around it that reaches its lows at the outskirts, then a somewhat empty buffer zone, and then a band of luxurious living that very quickly became very expensive, as it became a new safe haven for those rich who once resided in the downtown. From what I have seen, his city growth pattern happens in virtually every city around the world! Not only around Highway 80.

Eventually, the center of the city will get run down once again, sending yet another wave of the rich to the outskirts—but this time, the deterioration will take much longer than the first time around. This demise and revival in every city is cyclical, repeating in increasingly shorter intervals, until it reaches a point when the downtown is purely for offices, and no one really lives there. At that point, the city will enter a plateau of stability.

It appears that a center with a gravitational pool is the physical phenomenon that explains the social processes that shape human settlements. Their dynamics also reminds me of the Earth's magnetic field pattern, where the outside moves in to center, and the center moves out to the perimeter, in a repeating cycle.

Those who stay at the first band of poor outskirts are eternally under the spell of the center: their development is thwarted because of the overwhelming shortage of resources, which are constantly being sucked toward the center, in all spheres of life. The bigger the Chocolate Hill, the larger the radius, the worse it is for the most remote areas, at the very edges. Is there an escape from this vicious cycle? Of course! The answer is detaching from the orientation toward the original center, and creating your own new Chocolate Hill. As long as your new hill stays small enough, it will prosper and avoid the hideous cycle of urban reincarnation. Sometimes, when the outskirt communities are abandoned and forgotten for a while,— without the pressure from above, they burgeon into such thriving settlements, with their own new centers of culture.

San Francisco Bay Area is an example of both types of outskirters—those that are suppressed by identification with the center, which is San Francisco City, and those that have become their own new centers of life and culture. Although starkly different, Berkeley and Oakland are both thriving communities in the vicinity of San Francisco, who have managed to escape gravitational pool of the big city. Most other cities in that area are under the onus of San Francisco, and so exist in reference to it, which hinders their development.

It is the same with countries. With the creation of the European Union, many smaller countries have had to subjugate their cultural identities under the onus of one larger center—the governing Brussels. Even such large country as France has felt the pressure. Even though, the bigger the Chocolate Hill, the stronger its development potential, and abilities, large size comes with a price of suppressing the development of its peripheries. I remember, like it was yesterday, the farmers in Southern France complaining how, because of the European Union regulations, they could no longer grow lemons—and those were legendary lemons with aroma like nowhere else in the world, so good that even Italians came to get it, to make their Limoncello!

The funniest thing I realized about countries overall is that some of them act as a downtown of a city, and others—as an outside band for luxury living, or those who once worked in downtown, or are still commuting. Somehow, I can see the United States as the downtown of the world, where everyone goes to work and make money.

Around it—are its less affluent neighbors—Mexico, and even Canada in some respects, but the super rich move there to live, because they can afford a greater luxury for their money. Then, there is a super luxury band—the Caribbean. Of course, all of it is in flux, and nothing is clearcut. But—these are tendencies not to be overlooked!

What about the food in the boonies?

What puzzled me during my road trip across the United States was that in some middle-of-nowhere places, or the valleys between the Chocolate Hills, I would either find really great food, or food that was just awful. It happened so much that I was able to see a pattern. The good food I found was always in a place that was far enough and detached from any big center: it would stand on its own, a point, toward which people would come from far and wide. There could be other food places next to it, but not connected to it. The owners would refuse to move closer to any larger city center, and maintained their location in the middle of nowhere. Moving to the city center would mean higher rent, more traffic, more crime, more price competition—and that would be the pressure that a big Chocolate Hill wields on its member. Staying in the valley, far away from any Chocolate Hill would mean lower rent, no traffic, plenty of parking, and lower expenses —all of which would allow the business to provide a higher quality of product per dollar of cost. The customers would come there anyway, because the good deal, along with all of the luxuries of being away from the city, would be well worth the extra drive.

There were other food outlets that were on the outskirts, but still under the umbrella of a big city—and the food was not good. Those places appeared to exist in reference to the center and with its help, but not good enough to make it to the center. The very good ones in the middle of nowhere are often those who started on the outskirts, and then moved away farther away. It could also be that they moved to the center first, and then moved away into the luxury band of the city, and then further away.

No matter what each story of each good food outlet was, it is the autonomy and being away from the pressure of the city that they had in common. In the center of the city, we can find either really expensive high quality food, or cheap low quality food—each serving its market segment. The rich would go for the high quality, and the poor—for the low price. Anything in between, such as high quality cheap food, tends to either close business or move away from the center—to the luxury belt or to the middle of nowhere. The poor outskirts is usually not a viable option, because of the overall dire conditions there, lack of buying power, crime, and the looks of the area, which would not attract enough customers from far away. If such a move to the outskirts does happen, it is bound to lead to the gentrification of the area, and more businesses like it will eventually come that way.

Elsa, if you don't believe me, just trace the movement of businesses yourself, and you will see the proof of what I am saying! And there is more."

"I am starting to understand you. You are not insane, you are just a workaholic. Thinkaholic, yes, that's the word!"

"Thinking is my favorite sport, Elsa."

"Do you get cramps in your brain?"

"I will if I don't get out what I have to tell you."

"Mental constipation? I wouldn't wish that to my worst enemy."

"I am not your worst. Does that mean, I am in danger if I divulge?"

"Oh, no, by any means—splatter away! What was that thing about magnets?"

CATEGORIES AS MAGNETS

Nature knows no Friday, no rush hour, no last day of vacation. It has its own clock and calendar, and even then—it does not follow them.

—Meema Iselfanday

"Elsa, you are something else! Haven't you seen magnets before?"

"What about them?"

"Haven't you seen how they pull metal things toward them, as if with invisible strings?"

"Have you seen those strings?"

"I have felt them, which is as good, if not better, than seeing."

"Judging by the way it all behaves, a lot of stuff in the social space is made of metal!"

"Deus meus!"

"The social space is never clean-cut, but is always curvy, with categories flowing smoothly one into another, and where everything is on a continuum. The human mind does not tolerate ambiguity, and really wants to box in whatever object or idea it is considering into a clear category. The analogy of such mental categories in physical space is magnets, where anything metallic that is located between them is highly unstable, striving to cling to one magnet or the other. Those borderline zones between the two magnets are danger zones, as they cause much confusion and frustration for the human mind. They are zones of uncertainty. Interestingly, two categories with a dangerous middle looks like a reverse of a moderation curve, where the middle is optimal. The magnets model describes black-and-white thinking and intolerance of ambiguity, resulting both from mental laziness and a pressure to be efficient. It is a false dichotomy that feels so right, except that it is false. Here are a few examples, but those magnets are everywhere!"

Immune system: weak vs strong.

One's immune system can be rather weak or rather strong, but will show signs of fighting only in the zone between these two categories. An extremely weak immune system will allow a pathogen in, will not fight it, and the body will die from its attack. A very strong immune system will destroy the pathogen before it has a chance to settle in the body, and before a full immune system war is waged. In both cases, there will be few or none of the symptoms of a disease. An immune system that is neither very strong nor very weak will allow the pathogen to enter the body and will fight it with everything it has, manifesting itself in inflammation, auto-immune response, and other clear symptoms.

Air conditioners: cold vs mild climate.

A climate that is just right for the human body at all times is very rare. Tahiti may be one single place in the world, along with some other places in Polynesia. Otherwise, climates are mostly very cold or very hot or both. Some fall in those borderline ranges, where things get complicated. Living in a climate that is between really cold and just right for the human body is difficult, simply because of the decision to either invest into a major heating system. For a really cold climate, it is clearly a yes. For a climate that does not get cold enough, for enough days in a year—that is a tough decision to make. Is the investment worth it? Such places are found in coastal Australia and California. People here don't have central heating as they do in Europe, for example, and so often they live in the cold. In the winter, their room temperatures are on average colder than those in truly cold climates. They simply hold it through those cooler days.

Home heating: hot vs mild climate.

A climate between the normal and hot is also a problematic temperature range. Here, the people are puzzled over the decision of whether to invest into a major cooling system. The same people in coastal Australia and coastal California who weathered cooler days, will hold it through the hot days without an air conditioner. Simply because a few days of extreme heat in a year does not merit investing in a major air conditioner. Meanwhile, people in a truly hot climate, where hot days are the norm, will have invested into a major cooling system, and will not have to suffer the heat in their homes at all.

Climate zones: dry vs rainy.

Animals and even plants, living at the borderlines between climate zones have a more difficult time surviving, than those living a the center of each clearly developed climate. It is because in those climactic zones of uncertainty, where climate is unstable, the animals have to learn to adapt to more than one climate, in addition to expending energy on the adaptation itself. One manifestation of such an adaptation is animal migrations: they require great effort, and sometimes cost animals their lives!

Friends vs enemies.

Some people fall into a grey category of neither being a friend nor an enemy, and those people are possibly most harmful. With true friends, we are safe. With enemies —we have our weapons, and have our guards up. However, the potential harm of someone who is not exactly a friend nor an enemy is hard to estimate, because it is hard to know what to expect. Basically, we don't know what to do with them. It is best to turn such people into a sure friend, or consider them an enemy. Otherwise, one is better off avoiding them altogether. There is a reason that in the wild, a wounded animal is always killed—because it is far more dangerous than a normal happy predator. A harmless predator is a dead predator, as some people say.

Rich vs poor.

Crossing the border from poor to rich is the most exhilarating experience at first, and then—the most disheartening. At first, one's reference is the poor category, and getting enough money to be in the rich category feels like a great achievement, in relation to where one is coming from. Once one is finally considered rich, the reference category changes. Suddenly, one must compare themselves to the rest of the rich, and one finds that one is quite poor —relative to the rest of the people in the rich category. So, one is back to square one. Being somewhere on the borderline, neither poor nor really rich, is mentally taxing, the affiliation with a category is unstable, and people feel most volatile when they are in this area of transformation.

Interviews: right vs wrong candidate.

During the interviews, a candidate that seems clearly right will quickly be put into 'right' category. One who is clearly wrong for the job—will be put into the 'wrong' category, no more information needed. A candidate who cannot be easily understood is automatically rejected, and assigned into the 'wrong" category. This candidate might be simply something that the interviewer has never seen before, and might be, in fact, the best for the job. However, it is the limited knowledge, mental laziness and a habit of quick judgements that are so common among interviewers that can easily prevent the best candidate from getting the job. For the interviewer, it is much easier to sift the candidate into good, bad, and the other—the other being thrown into the bad pile, without going deeper and examining an unusual candidate. This is a perfect example of black-and-white thinking, and an intolerance of ambiguity and grey areas.

Culture: insider vs outsider.

Someone who is not yet fully accepted into a group, and is no longer a guest, is at the worst position possible. Someone who is part of us has the rights and privileges of our group, and guests also have their guest rights. When you overstay your time as a guest, you lose your guest privileges, not yet having earned those that go with being an insider. In addition, if you decide to leave the group, you lose the insider privileges, without any hope of gaining those that come with a status of a guest, any time soon. Immigration and tourism, as well as families and gangs, and any differentiated groups of people are social spaces where this pattern is found. As long as there is an 'us' and 'them', there is the transitory area of social discomfort that everyone must pass through before becoming part of 'us.'

Personality: superior vs inferior.

This is a personal peeve! Authoritarian personality comes with an inability to relate to others as equals, and a tendency to either classify the other person as inferior or superior. Such psychological malfunction is correlated with the personality disorder of Narcissism, and is widely spread, the duality in behavior often being disguised as a reaction to circumstances, instead of one's social inadequacy. People with authoritarian personality are very susceptible to borderlines.

The more authoritarian someone's personality is, the less tolerance they will have with someone else's equality, the more they will be pressed to put labels on people and events, the more black-and-white their thinking is, the more they will oppress their subordinates, and the more they will kiss up to their bosses. Authoritarian personality is one the most harmful attributes in the workplace. It stifles progress, when those who have it choose their most talented subordinates as scapegoats, which causes brain drain when those subordinates leave the company. It also distorts the real picture to make it appear much better than it is, when those with authoritarian personality give reports to their bosses on how the company is doing. What businesses really need to do is test potential employees for authoritarian personality. If you have someone like that in your family—I am sorry. I feel your pain.

Changing lanes: slow vs fast.

Changing lanes is like a dance between the two drivers! Driving timidly, you would mostly end up pulling in behind the car that is already there, when changing into that lane. If you try to change lanes faster and more aggressively, the other driver will most likely give in, because for them—that is not the fight they are willing to fight. However, if you try to change lanes in the most civilized and cautious way—that will most often get the other driver to speed up and block you from pulling into their lane and going in front of them, making you mad.

Showing off: rich vs poor.

Have you noticed that the very rich do not show off their wealth? If you have not noticed, you will, if you look into it. The very poor, also do not show it off, since they don't have it. The volatile and anxious middle of the socio-economic scale has the most potential to move up socially and the most desire to show off what they have. Not that everyone in this space will do so, but only that those who do show off—usually do not come from the top rich or the bottom poor.

Humor: jokes vs insults.

Jokes are funny, insults are painful. But what happens when you hear a mean joke, so mean that you would say that it is really an insult, only disguised as a joke? Jokes are often used as a sneaky tool to insult somebody. You say your insult, and coat it with a joke, and here we go —it is just a joke, why would anyone be mad? The other person is framed in a lose-lose situation, it is a total zugzwang! No matter how they answer, they look bad: either accepting of the offense, or considered to have no sense of humor. The zone of uncertainty between a joke and a plain insult is sometimes used as a reverse Straw man fallacy, where the jokes sets up the other person to look like they are misinterpreting the joke, by interpreting it as an insult.

Relationships: friends vs lovers.

Great grief about the uncertainty in relationships will always be immortalized in literature, over and over again. Why? Because it is so painful. The borderline zone of uncertainty between someone's being either your friend or a lover is one of the greatest anxiety sources for people. Whether you love the other person or not, you always want to know where you stand, so that you know how to be with them. That strong pull to know, one way or another, is a sure sign of the magnets model of categories being in play.

Texts: serious vs facetious.

Playing with categories is often found in literature and published speech, especially all that is meant for entertainment, and this style of presentation is creeping into everything else—because everything is under an increasing pressure to entertain. So, an example would be a scientist talking of potential dangers of Artificial Intelligence to humanity, and then saying that humanity needs something to 'save their arse.'

This is an extreme example, but it is a familiar technique, both jarring and funny—exactly for the reason that it is in the uncertainty zone of being neither fully serious, neither fully comedic. Actually, it gets tricky here. If one is clearly established in a serious genre, an occasional joke is pleasant. Too many jokes would make it hard to understand whether one could take it seriously, and places the whole presentation into the danger zone between genres, when it is no longer clear what the genre is, and by what rules it goes. On the other hand, if a comedic text or speech includes too many serious thoughts and statements, it will also enter the uncertainty zone, and no one will laugh. Of course, the social context will be the best heuristic for what the genre is meant to be, but that will not solve the problem of discomfort that an inter-genre presentation creates.

Appreciation: nice vs nasty.

Someone gives you a piece of your favorite chocolate. Is this that mean co-worker that never says hi, or is it your usual buddy who sits and talks to you every day? That makes a big difference. If you are generally a nice person, doing something nice is not appreciated greatly, but is rather expected, if not taken for granted. If you are generally not nice to others, doing a tiny nice thing will be met with great surprise and appreciation. It will be over-valued and disproportionately over-appreciated, in reference to the category in which people see you—the nasty one. If you are not really nasty and neither really nice, and you do a nice thing—people will not know how to understand it, and might not trust your good intentions. They might think you just need something from them, and so you are bribing them, setting them up for a return of favor. The paradox here is that the act is the same in all cases, but its interpretation depends on the category of reference. It follows the law of magnets!

Fashion: conservative vs rebellious.

Why is it so bewildering to a fashion outsider, what the fuss in fashion is all about? How do we know when something is matching, and something is clashing? There are many rules in the game of fashion. One of them is about not mixing those rules. Mixing rules in a single piece is a perfect definition of a clash and a lack of taste. So, we can take Rocker Chic style on one hand, and Vintage style on the other. If a person goes to a conservative gathering, where people expect to see a clear style of clothing, dressing half and half in each style will guarantee a social disaster. That is the area between the two categories, that special danger zone. If one perfectly follows the rules of either style, clearly belonging to one single category, then the social reception will be positive.

Every rule has an exception, and so does the rule of not mixing rules. If the rule is a rebellion, a chaos, an anarchy that is hoped to bring forth a whole that is greater than the sum of its parts. To signal good taste, a mixed style has to have the audience that is expecting being shocked and surprised by a new mixture of rules, and an audience that focuses on clothing as a serious subject matter. So, when a minimalist style of Japanese subdued colors is mixed with Indian jewelry and body art in a deliberately rebellious and surprising way—we might get something interesting, even though they are quite opposite. It is all about how it is done, and most of such experimentation is an aesthetic fiasco, and it is what inundates the market in the 21 century. Anyone in fashion will tell you that, anyone.

Hair color: platinum blond vs white.

This is about the difference between being extremely blond and having all white hair caused by age. If a young person colors their hair blond to the point of being white, the young face will not allow it to snap into the category of grey hair. If the face is old, bleaching hair to the point of being virtually white will be perceived as white hair caused by old age. The hair is exactly the same in the two cases, but it is the face that serves as a reference category and tells us how to interpret the color—bleach blond or old white.

The borderline area here is found when medium to dark hair on an middle age person is bleached to being very close to completely white, or if the hair naturally looses pigment due to some physical condition. It might create mental confusion and discomfort, since the age does not provide a clear category for reference, in order to decide whether the person's hair became white too early, or they have an extremely bleached hair color and are at the point of becoming too old for this kind of a bleached style. There is an exception, where a middle aged person maintains a funky style, reflected in their clothing,—all of which together will serve as a reference and an explanation of why their hair is so white.

The uncanny valley: film vs animation.

When animation is done in a hyper-realistic style, it approaches the category of film. As long as it is perceived in reference to the animation category, it is greatly admired for its detail and realisticity of experience. The danger zone is where animation becomes so realistic that it starts crossing over into the film category, and is being now judged in reference to film. Hyper-realistic animation is a poor imitation of reality, if judged in reference to film category, and causes the viewer to experience contempt, instead of amazement. The uncomfortable confusion caused by the ambiguity of attachment to categories is what is called uncanny valley.

Reality: magic realism vs surrealism.

Magical realism is based on reality, stretching it toward the magical and the impossible. Surrealism is not based on reality, but on the magic, the mysterious, and the inexplicable of the mind and imagination—which is then stretched toward reality and is illustrated in the familiar terms derived from the commonly understood reality. If not clearly presented, the two can be confused and easily misjudged.

Offenders: slight vs extreme.

When someone is a little bit offensive, the reactions are more intense than when they are intensely offensive. Shouldn't the fight reaction increase proportionately, as the offender gets meaner? The more someone is offending me, the more I defend myself, right? In fact, the reactions look counterintuitive. When offenders reach a certain threshold of attack intensity, they are suddenly perceived as being in a different, more dangerous category,—too dangerous to fight against, so they get avoided instead of faced in combat. So, sometimes, when you want to say something harsh, it is better not to pose yourself as a nice person being guilty about saying such a thing. That immediately anchors you into a soft opponent category, and people will readily attack back. If you pose yourself as a harsh person, from the beginning, then follow up in a harsh way, the people will surprisingly not attack you as much and give in faster. In addition, you will be pardoned for being harsh, because that is what people expect of you anyway, because of your harsh nature. That is often inexplicable and seemingly unfair to those who try to be nice, and get attacked much worse than a harsh person, for the same offense.

Products: Italian fashion vs comfort food.

These are two different categories for positioning a product, in order to appeal to the buyer. Italian Fashion type of products is just like Italian fashion—refined, chic, and glamorous, and the examples are fine Italian clothes, haute couture, and filigree traditional jewelry. The other type—Comfort Food—feels like comfort food from home, from an innocent place in childhood where all was well, and is all about feeling safe, comfortable, and even childlike. Hyggelig is the word here. A good example of that is Ugg shoes. No one could walk around in those pajama-like wide fur slippers on steroids, unless they were positioned in the Comfort Food category, where they simply shine! Ugg would be considered ugly, if judged in reference to the Italian Fashion category, and nobody would buy them.

If products send ambiguous messages and do not clearly signal to belong to one single category, they are at risk of failure. That is why, for example, anything in the

Comfort Food category should not look overly beautiful, so as not get confused with Italian Fashion. Look at the babies in a movie, where they play victims and need to inspire the viewer to save them. In order to incite the maternal instinct in the viewer, the children should not look angelic and glamorous, but should miss a few baby teeth, and generally be endearingly gawkish—then we want to save them. Sorry for the cynicism! When children are from the Italian Fashion category—they can be found in child beauty pageants, and instead of endearment, suggest a POV of a pedophile, unfortunately.

Anything that rebels against either of these two categories—it better be done with passion and gusto, so as to be clearly seen as rebellious, in reference to a specific category. So, if a model wears jeans with tears in them, they must be placed in a setting that invokes the Italian Fashion category, which is an extreme opposite of torn clothes. If the model is placed in a hometown down-to-earth context, where the tears would be seen as a natural wear and tear, the rebellion would be cancelled out, and the fashion effect —a fiasco.

Ratings: cheap and expensive.

We use ratings as a system of guidance for virtually all products and services. Using the same rating system for two different categories of products tends to misrepresent the actual quality and value of the product. What is interesting is that we never know how good something is in an absolute sense, just by looking at its rating, because quality of a product is rated as a ratio of the expected value to its price, and often expectations for cheap vs expensive categories play a trick on our minds.

Just take the case of hotels. The problem with expectations is that they are based on our imagination of how a hotel should be, for the price they are charging, whereas not every traveler has had a chance to sample a statistically large enough number of hotels in this price category to really have a reasonable expectation. So, the quality for the price point is completely a product of our imagination of what a certain price should represent, which then determines our rating. It often happens with hotels that are on the borderline between really cheap and really expensive. Any hotel in this borderline category is better off being included in the lower category: big fish in a small pond. We tend to give such hotels a rave review, if they are placed in a lower price category, where our expectations are lower. This very same hotel will get much lower ratings, if placed in a higher price category, because now it will be rated in reference to all the other expensive hotels. It is better to be a pricier hotel with high quality ratings in a cheap hotel category, than a cheaper hotel with low quality ratings, in a category of expensive hotels. The quality and the price of the hotel is exactly the same, but the ratings are drastically different, and this is where lies the ratings misrepresentation.

Moreover, our frustration with borderline price and quality is so great that we take it out on our exaggeration of ratings: good becomes excellent, and bad becomes terrible. Often, people will not even rate a hotel if their impression is somewhere in the middle.

Envy: amateur vs professional.

This is about comparing yourself to others. If we see ourselves in the same category as the other person, then all their attributes are a subject to comparison. If we see ourselves as being in different categories, differences are expected, and so, generally, envy does not arise. So, for example, if someone is presented to us as famous singer, saying that their voice is divine, and we sing only in the shower, we will not feel threatened, and will not automatically compare ourselves to them, just because the difference is so great that we see them in a different category altogether. Even if we would love to be a singer superstar, we do not feel intensely bad hearing that this famous singer's voice is divine. That's right, that is why they are a famous singer, and having a divine voice is expected.

On the other hand, if we were a professional singer, aspiring to fame, and were introduced to another aspiring professional singer, and somebody said that their voice is divine—that would really hurt. What if we were just a student in voice, not yet professional? In that situation, we would unconsciously decide whether to compete or not with this famous singer with a divine voice, based on what category pulls us stronger: are we closer to the amateur category or to the professional one? This very decision will determine whether we envy this person or not, and whether the comment about their divine voice hurts us.

This happens because we are magnetically drawn to categories, and the most volatile place to be is somewhere on the cusp between two, where categories tear us apart, as if with a magnetic pull. So, the closer we get to the threshold of being a professional singer, the better we feel about ourselves—because we still consider ourselves an amateur— but look how close we are to a professional! As soon as we step over that threshold and consider ourselves a professional, we can no longer compare ourselves to other amateurs. Now, our reference is based on an average professional singer, and we suddenly find ourselves not as great and successful anymore, in relation to this higher standard.

One quick solution to this state of grief is simply re-classifying ourselves as still an amateur, entering the professional world—and feel instantly better. It allows us to re-live stepping over the threshold for the first time, and remember the exhilaration. Although, this rationalization might be a dangerous avoidance of reality. If one really wants to become a professional, one must face the challenge of a raised bar, and treat it as an inspiration rather than a threat to self-esteem. Hsiu! That was mouthfull! Why don't you say something, Elsa?"

"You told me to be quiet and listen."

"But how would I know that you are listening, if you are not saying anything? You know, listening is a selfish skill, if you give nothing back."

"I slept through the whole thing. What you said was fascinating, though! I can see the negative symmetry between curves and categories, and thought of a million more examples, which I will not mention."

"So, you heard everything, Elsa?"

"I dreamt of it all. Now what?"

"Next is the tabu subject, the original sin."

"That's a change!"—laughed Elsa.

"But I can't talk about it, because you wouldn't listen."

"That's because I am not selfish."

"You got it all wrong: you need to listen and then say something that makes sense. That's all!"

"Then you, yes you, have to say something that makes sense. So far so good. But what about the original sin?"

"What about it?"

PLEASURE, REDEFINED

Everything is instrumental to happiness.

—*Meema Iselfanday*

"There is nothing original, Vera."

"Say what?"

"There is nothing original about the original sin. Are you hard of hearing?"

"Only when it serves a good purpose. Well, they say, I was born a sinner. Let me tell you, I was not born a sinner! This whole idea is the ultimate control tool to make me do what you want, and not what I want. Nothing else! Do you see?"

"I din't even think of thinking that! Relax, Vera, I am not trying to control you, or even make you feel guilty. I just want to understand you, and you don't know who you really are, until you find your happiness. Or your pleasure in life."

"I will not understand myself until you do. That is why I keep talking to you."

"That is why I keep listening,"—said Elsa. I smiled, —a smile is a tiny messenger of pleasure,—and kept talking.

"Pleasure is what our life is all about! That is why pleasure is even stronger than fear. We survive because we are all good donkeys: we run after a carrot and flea from a stick. It is like one magnet pulls us and another one repels us, creating all motion that there is. Fear helps us avoid danger, but pleasure tells us what to do. We would be lost without it, we wouldn't want to live, because we wouldn't have a reason to live. Suicide happens when life no longer is a source of pleasure. Between life and death, it is death that seems more pleasurable. Depression is nothing but learned helplessness in the pursuit of pleasure."

"How macabre, Vera!"

"Ah, it is certainly not. Death is only meant to make us understand that pleasure is not the original sin, but the reason we are born at all. Pleasure is sacred. However, pleasure of someone caring is different from pleasure of an egoist, and there lies the original sin—in the intention. If life is not about pleasure and happiness, what is the point?"

"Notice, you have pleasure and happiness as two separate words. There are other things besides pleasure that make life worth living."

"Like what?"

"Like finding the love of your life. Like loving your children. Like looking at the stars in the night sky and feeling the joy run down your spine, just from the realization of how much greater they universe is than a mere human—a tiny powerless speck, sending hope up into the unknown. Like climbing a hill, reaching the summit, and when no one is around, screaming your lungs out into the sky! Ah, some people enjoy their money and their power. Some perverts enjoy hurting others. Others experience intense joy by seeing others happy!"

"There is the rub! If all of that is not pleasure, than, I am a Peruvian goat."

"You are a Peruvian goat!"—Elsa opened her eyes, as if in support of what she was saying, and closed them again.

"The thing is, Elsa, everything that is good in this life—it is all pleasure. Happiness is a special kind of pleasure—a pleasure that appeals to the best of what we are. The more developed someone is, the more sophisticated, awe-inspiring, and beneficial to others their pleasure is. Pleasure from harming someone is what we call sin, because, if you look at the big picture—there is more hurt in it than pleasure. That is how pleasure has become synonymous with hurt: too much harm has been done in the name of pleasure.

Just think about it! Who in our history decided that pleasure is bad and sinful? Those who have dealt with with the worst of the worst. Yet, there is so much more to it. Pleasure does not have to be sensual, it can be mental, emotional, even moral! Most of us would experience great pleasure in planting a tree and knowing that it would help saving the planet, or saving a stranded dog and finding it a new home. That's pleasure too!"

"I am liking what I hear. It gives me mental pleasure. Go on."

"We generally take it for granted that everyone wants to live: simply because it feels good. What else is there besides living? Death, as an alternative, is so null that it is not even a meaningful option. Have you thought about it? Death means nothing at all, if one has not been alive first. One cannot die without living."

"True. And?"

Pleasure as a guideline for living.

"And, it is interesting that it is only when living no longer brings the expected pleasure that humans start asking themselves about the meaning of life. One does not wonder about meaning when one is happy. Happiness is yet

67

another type of pleasure. Only in the moments when living becomes painful, we consider death. Death is not a pro-death choice, but anti-life. Death is like breaking up with a lover who has been hurting you for too long, looking for another. Except, there is no other life to go to, we only have one. The only real choice we have is fighting for pleasure. Death means no choices, it is the ultimate lack of freedom.

Pleasure is the language of nature, to tell us what to do and how to be, and we wouldn't have a clue without it. As children, we learn all of the ways to get pleasure from life, exploring all the intricate books and crannies of their surroundings, discovering every nuance of pleasure sources. A child knows no sin. What makes something sinful is a judgment, but not the act itself, or the experience of pleasure. A pleasure can only be judged as sinful if it causes someone else experience pain—or robs someone else their pleasure. That is all! It is all circumstantial and secondary. There is nothing, absolutely nothing sinful, evil or even faintly bad, about pleasure. Without pleasure as a guideline, we wouldn't be human."

"Without it, even animals wouldn't be animals, nor plants would be plants."

Sources of pleasure.

"Seeing pleasure in a very narrow and primitive sense, and the denial of it, is what has led our civilization astray and made us generally unhappy. There are so many sources of pleasure, and it is a question of choice, not of outright denial. Pleasure is an art worth mastering, an art worth dedicating one's life to—in all of its myriad of varieties. Even more—we should be taught how and where to derive pleasure in life, in healthy ways. It is a cultural wisdom that should be passed on from generation to generation, pleasure being venerated as a sacred force of life. Unfortunately, we grow up in a sweeping denial of pleasure, and in the absence of its understanding. And so, we are pushed toward the worst of it: drugs, promiscuity, violence,—that which is most immediately available and requires no learning. And so, there comes a confirmation that pleasure is bad. Do you see the vicious cycle here?"

"I think that, in denying pleasure, the religious dogma has denied us our right to exist. Without giving us a carrot, it has used its stick to run us down into a corner of despair and loss of all meaning in life. Instead of teaching us how to be a more beautiful human being, and instead of cherishing all the different types of pleasure, it has denied us the right for it. It has denounced nature itself!"—murmured Elsa.

"And how should one live, for what, if pleasure is a bad thing?"

"I guess, someone needs us to believe that, so they can supplant our innate pleasure instincts with their own mental framework, where we are only tools for achieving their goals. And their own pleasure."

"Probably, just power over us,"—I said.

"I am sad to think of how much of my life has gone by in feeling guilty. Just generally guilty, for no good reason. Sometimes, I wondered why I was born. I thought maybe I should not have been born at all, if this life is nothing but a train of suffering, where feeling good is frowned upon. What a senseless, senseless world!"

"Elsa, I was glad you listened, but when you talked! Ah, just thank you."

Types of pleasure.

"Let's see, Vera, what kinds of pleasure do we have?"

"Well, we have our five senses, and each comes with a slew of possibilities. Then, our sixth sense in the brain.

Now that! That is where it all happens, and this is where all types of pleasure get their ability to make us happy."

"Emotions! Love, friendship, books, films, music, nature! Emotion is everywhere, and it is all about pleasure!"—Elsa opened her eyes and looked straight at me.

"I think, the guideline for understanding pleasure is in wishing others well. The awe we can experience at the sight of something beautiful, be it a person, a story, or the sunrise—it is the primal instinct that allows us to discern between good and bad, and between pleasure that can harm or heal."

"How funny! It is love your neighbor as yourself, after all. It is in seeing the big picture, the world beyond the tip of your nose. It is about how your own pleasure effects the right for pleasure of others. And you cannot wish anyone well, you cannot experience the awe, until you accept the rest of the world as an indelible part of yourself,"—said Elsa, staring into space.

"This is where mental type of pleasure comes in. It is in the sudden eureka moments of truth. When truth feels like the absolute knowledge of something, without ever touching it."

"It is not all about the physical pleasures that people think of first, there is so much more. I think, the more a

71

person develops, the more sources of pleasure open themselves to them. I personally always feel high on life. So much so that I don't know what to do with myself—there are too many things that make me feel euphoric!"

Pleasure and drugs.

"I guess, life is the ultimate drug!"—I said and looked at Elsa, then she nodded, reminding me of the welcoming cat that you can see at the Japanese store fronts. I continued: "Sometimes, the slightest touch of someone's hand can send a shower of goosebumps all over one's body —no medical drugs necessary. No wonder, love is called a drug. A song can sometimes reach to the very core of you, so deep, you did not know that place even existed. The smell of fresh rain hitting the ground, petrichor, can trigger a feel like being held by someone you love. A certain smell can send your mind flying to the distant lands you left years ago, and make you see images of people you have completely forgotten. A eureka moment can be experienced so intensely that you feel like your body is made of pure light, and gravity exists no longer. Someone's casual comment can launch a string of ideas that reaches far into your brain and scratches the itch that bothered you for years, like that long itch stick with a little hand at the end of it."

"I am too tired to disagree with you for the sake of disagreeing, so I will agree with you, Vera, and say this: everything that a medical drug can make people feel, they are born to feel naturally. Drugs violate people, much like a tsunami comes and levels a whole city, where only a little whiff of air was all that was necessary to set a puffy dandelion seed flying."

"Too bad, people use substances and pay to experience what is already there in them by nature, for free!"

"It is like paying for the right to breathe! Of course, it is the monetization of everything, the biggest mass deception of our civilization!"—said Elsa, and I bumped her chair with my foot.

"Oh, I see, that is why they need the dogma! To convince us that we cannot feel pleasure on our own because that is bad, oh so bad. Then, they sell the pleasure to us in capsules of joy, only to point out how weak and sinful we are, since we can't resist."

"The biggest and most cynical conspiracy of all times!"—said Elsa and squinted her eyes, as if I were one of the conspirators.

"You know what lets them manipulate us? It is our duality of body and mind. The body feels one thing, but the mind cancels out all the pleasure. This probably evolved as a mechanism to prevent us from hurting others in our pursuit of pleasure, but it also works against us, when we buy into artificial expectations. For example, we are healthy, we are safe, have food and shelter, we have friends and family, and everything around us is at peace. Yet, we are not satisfied. We want more: more money, more power—more than we naturally need. Maybe a promotion, maybe something that somebody else has. Who was it who said that we work at the jobs we don't like, in order to buy things we don't need, in order to impress people we don't care about? Something like that. You get the idea!"

"False expectations, needs that are not really there. That is how they get us!"

"Who is they?"

"You know. And I know. Everyone knows."

"What do they want from us?"

"They want us to have cravings for pleasures we don't naturally have. It is like a drug dealer who starts people on drugs to get them addicted, so they will come asking for more, and so that they would do anything to get their next dose,"—I said, looking at my feet, as if this was where I got all my thoughts.

"What are they getting out of it?"

"Power. Power to keep us working and making them money. Like farmed animals."

"Or, what if this gigantic machine of artificial pleasure is the only way to progress? Although, you heard the fisherman's story, right? About a man who was a poor fisherman, until he went and became a lawyer to get more money and have a better life. When he finally retired, he went back to fishing. Very funny! So, what's the physical process that describes the social phenomenon of pleasure?"

Physical counterparts of pleasure.

"Well, the farm was one. I guess, there is not much about curves in pleasure. But pleasure is about push and pull, and adding pluses and minuses, to get the overall value. There is a definite physical counterpart in what happens to us when we are torn apart by multiple sources of pleasure, like if you have a turtle, a fish, and an eagle pull a cart, all at the same time! This causes instability, confusion, and indecision in people's actions and desires, and makes us think that life is too complicated."

"Life is complicated, if you try to figure it all out. If you just follow your pleasure instinct, you have no questions to ask."

"Oh, it is not so simple! Our sources of pleasure do contradict each other."

A few pleasure opposites.

"Well, they do, but deep down, you always know what's right for you. Right?"

"Let me just list some examples of these opposing pairs of pleasure, and then we shall see. Here we go:

Conservation vs change.

People hate change, you know that! But they also grow weary of routine.

Creation vs destruction.

People delight in constructing their own home, and they also savor destroying beautifully designed desserts.

Fear of the unknown vs curiosity.

We fear the unknown, xenophobia is real. At the same time, we do have this inner call for adventures! Fernweh is real, too.

Staying at home vs being outside.

We love cuddling in the safety of home. That also can feel claustrophobic, and so we yearn for being outside, in the open spaces.

Familiarity vs novelty.

We love being around familiar people and things. We also love to explore and be surprised!

These are all about minuses and pluses, cancelling each other. The sources of pleasure are like vectors, sticking in different directions, and somehow we need to add them up to decide where to go."

"I loved your example about travel. You must be dreaming of being elsewhere."

"I am already elsewhere, Elsa!"

"But, there are so many more examples you forgot to mention!"

"I will let you finish them in your head. You got the idea. Oh, by the way, not all sources of pleasure are created equal."

"Who would disagree? Dancing and singing develops hearing and coordination, as well as an aesthetic sense, to name a few. What does alcohol improve in a person?"

"Going back to pleasure monetization as a culprit for our inability to find pleasure naturally. In any developed society, monetization of pleasure is only possible if people are taught to forget that all the best things in life are free. If people believe that all pleasure is to be paid for, they will do anything for money. This way of living is spreading to primitive societies via globalization. Have you seen the movie 'The Gods Must be Crazy'? It's an old one, but it explains everything."

"Everything is enough for me."

The culture of alcohol.

"In the west, there is barely a social venue without alcohol these days. What a perfect money-sucking tool! Alcohol may not be a known source of pleasure in a remote Polynesia village, but it could be slowly adopted via exposure to it, through direct human contact or via media. If the alcohol consuming culture is perceived as superior in some other ways—more developed, for example,—the adoption of alcohol as a pleasure source is even more rapid. The problem is that it replaces and stigmatizes other healthier sources of pleasure as less cool and old-fashioned. The risk is not just that drinking kava in Fiji could be replaced with drinking alcohol, but ritual dancing and singing could fall victim to the new sources pleasure, for which the locals would have to pay, locking themselves into a dependency on the monetary system."

"Going against the system? I would feel like Atlas, holding the whole world on my shoulders. Sorry. I do get bitter sometimes, but that's because I am generally bitter."

"Then what makes you keep on living?"

"You know what the real original sin is? It is that we are born with equal rights, but without equal abilities to experience pleasure. So, why do I live? Life for me is a game—the source of pleasure you didn't even mention."

"Game? It is the mechanics of all human behavior, the ultimate and the only vehicle of pleasure delivery to every human cell!"

"I gather, it is not the game that you think I would be thinking of."

"I wouldn't think that you would think that I thought you were thinking that, Elsa."

"Is this a game?"

"Not the game you thought I thought you were thinking of."

"Oh, stop it, Vera!"

"You play that game just like everyone else. That is why your name is Elsa."

"That is not why my name is Elsa! But what game is it?"

THE GAME INSTINCT

If you cannot win in a game, question its rules.
                                        —Meema Iselfanday

"It's a mind game, without which no mind can function."

"What is it?"

"You cannot enjoy playing a game unless you know the rules of it. You can't enjoy it if you don't play it, or if you don't know it exists. You cannot get carried away playing Hnefatafl, unless you know what that is!"

"What's Hnefatafl? Did you just make that up?"—elsa wrinkled her nose, turned her whole body toward me, and lowered one brow. She looked ridiculous.

"You look ridiculous, you know that? It's an ancient Viking game."

"Why would I care?"

"Precisely my point."

"Well, now I do care!"

"Just like conservation of energy in physics, there is energy in people that needs to be spent, otherwise they turn to violence. This energy feels like motivation. The more drive we have, the more alive we are, medically speaking. We are wired to spend this energy on challenges that line

81

our way to pleasure, and we love the challenge just as much as we love our goal. That is why the more something costs us—the more we love it in the end. Finally, rewards and punishments are a nonverbal way of telling us whether we won. And so, life goes on."

"Can you be more specific?"

"Sure, but I prefer to stay abstract. It lulls my brain into sleep. I can talk in my sleep, you know!"

"And I can only listen in my sleep. We are a good match, Vera, rien à dire!"

"Ok, so in physical terms, a social game we are talking about is like playing tennis with someone, where the ball is served and then it comes back. Not much more to it, at first glance. But, this is where it gets interesting. Knowing how people seek control over their environment through engaging in all sorts of games makes it easy to manipulate them. A single desire—and you got them by their neck. An average person does not seek out a game to play, but buy into a game that society, or family—or whoever—offers them. Then, you really got them hooked! Jobs, families, schools, neighborhoods, even professions and social identities—they are all obvious systems of rules one enters, they are the game. Not only do these games tell us what the rules are, but they also provide us with the goals, essentially dictating what pleasure is and what we want, as if we couldn't think for ourselves. Games are boxes we live in, they define our entire worldview, and we live inside them, as if buried alive. Once a human being buys into a game, there is virtually no force strong enough to get them out of there! This is why it is so hard to get people out of religious sects—those are games of rules they bought into!"

"Really, I need more specifics on what you mean by a game."

"Like its anatomy? It does not have arms and legs, I'll tell ya'! But, yes, sure, ok, fine. Here it is. There are six basic components in any game."

Anatomy of a game.

Azart.

Azart is a Russian word, without a literal equivalent in English. It roughly translates as excitement, but it is much more than that. Azart is a special type of excitement, it is an intense feeling of being ready and brave to face any challenge, believing yourself to be a sure winner, and tasting the victory in one's mouth before it has actually happened. It is really the energy that signifies that one is well and alive, and is ready to face life's challenges.

Azart is what we generally call drive, motivation, enthusiasm, or even will. Azart is sometimes used self-destructively, as in gambling and addictions. However, it is the energy necessary to engage in a game, in wanting to meet the challenge, and in order to achieve the goal.

In fact, azart is the other face of adrenaline, and thus is a great solution to stage freight. If one mentally reframes everything stressful as a game, including a stage performance, adrenaline will be channelled into azart, and will work for you instead of against you.

Goals.

As long as one possesses the azart, one is quite eager to engage in any available game, just as a newly born baby instinctively searches for the mother's breast. In playing piano, the goal is to become the best piano player. In having children, the goal is to become the best parents. In being a church-goer, one will be the most exemplary one. It is engrained in us that all goals in games are instrumental to feeling good, and so we are vulnerable to manipulation. We might not like the whole game, but if we are in—all goals are good now. So, if one starts working for a corporation producing tobacco, the cognitive dissonance is often overpowered by the sheer presence of the corporation's goals, which are undeniably harmful. Joining a gang makes it much easier to commit crimes one couldn't even think about otherwise. How about becoming the best drug dealer? Once someone buys into the game of dealing drugs, one will invest great effort to become good at it, even though the activity as a whole is obviously morally rejected by the society.

It is interesting how in film, the viewers can be passionately siding with the villain, as long as the villain has an obstacle to overcome, and we buy into the villain's game —no matter how odious the villain is. One of the immediate goals in film is to make the audience identify with its characters. If the villain has a problem—we are there to empathize and try to overcome the obstacle vicariously. This is how susceptible we are to games! We really do wish for the criminal to get away with robbing a bank, and even a killer to get away with murder, just for the sake of overcoming the challenge. Only then do we want the justice served, but not before winning of the game of chase and flee.

Rules.

Any single activity in which humans engage has rules. The rules of each game are sometimes self-evident, as in friendship, for example. Friendship is a game, in the sense that there are things one would do to make it work, and there are things that can destroy it. Many games have complicated rules that one must learn, yet others—have unwritten rules that one has to discover for one's self.

So, in friendship, the rules are so instinctual that one might think there are no rules at all. In the game of chess, one absolutely must learn the rules. Check mate is not self-evident. The particular etiquette of a place, rituals, traditions, and practices in a specific culture—all must be learned. Many of them are unwritten and are learned by observing and copying others. For example, how low to bow in Japan or how hard to shake one's hand in a western society, is not something that every child is necessarily taught. Children just learn it in action.

Rules provide the context for the challenges of a game, and tell the participant what is relevant and what is not. So for example, in the west, showing the sole of one's foot does not have much significance. In India, on the other hand, it can destroy an important relationship, without any words being spoken. To get accepted into a good university, one must perform well academically, but what clothes and makeup one wears on the daily basis to school—is quite irrelevant, at least directly. In order to become the healthiest person in the world, smoking and drinking alcohol are a definite no-no. However, to a politician—it is not part of the rules of a political game. One could be a smoker and a very successful president. Meanwhile, one could be a terrible public speaker and be one of the healthiest people on the planet. Enough examples!

Challenge.

A challenge in a game is the obstacle one must overcome, in order to win and get to the goal, which then promises to bring pleasure—physical, emotional, intellectual, and so on. A challenge must follow the rules, or is described by the rules. So, if the game is to learn to scuba dive, one would not be training to scuba dive by washing the oxygen tanks, obviously! One will not become the best scuba diver by brushing their teeth either.

Ridiculous, isn't it? It is only ridiculous because it is so extreme of an example. But take, for instance, teaching profession as a game. Learning empathy has not been part of the course curriculum in teacher education, so it is sometimes seen as secondary, or even irrelevant. Is it relevant as a rule for reaching a goal of being a good teacher? In my mind, it certainly is, but for many old school teachers—they get along without it just fine. So, in every game, the rules might not be clear, and the challenges might be overlooked, as well as the goals might be interpreted incorrectly, and there simply could be many versions of a game. What is a good teacher? There are as many answers as there are teachers.

Once the definition of a challenge is agreed upon, one can enter the game and wait for the challenge to appear. Unless a game is a controlled simulation, the challenges in any game are unpredictable. This is where azart waxes its strength, pumping adrenaline into our system. The unpredictability of challenges is the main driver of our addiction to games, and of our azart. Looking for the news is a classical example of a challenge, in a very vague game of being up to date. The reason people get easily addicted to social media, and any source of communication, and even to going to work, is the unpredictability that gives them the drive they need to continue living. Too much unpredictability can wear one out, but generally—it is the greatest stimulant our life can offer.

This is why performances, including playing an instrument, all competitions, and even art exhibits, are all so exciting. It is not because we have never played that certain piano piece, or have not seen our own painting, but because we have not seen the reaction of audience to what we produce, and its unpredictability is exciting. For the audience, who have not seen anything yet, any show is automatically exciting. This is where the term spoiler comes from! God forbid you show the whole plot in the movie trailer—barely anyone would want to see the whole movie. If you tell someone the ending of a film beforehand—do it at your own risk. Challenges are all about unpredictability.

Response.

Response is simply the response to the challenge in the game. Call-and-response is as old as humanity itself. It is found in tribal songs, in all conversations, in all relationships.

Feedback.

Feedback is the reward or punishment that the participants receives, as a result of meeting the challenge. It tells the participant whether the goal has been reached, and whether the response the participant offered was on the right track. Often, the response is a trial-and-error that slowly shapes the understanding of the game's rules and goals.

"Elsa, our game instinct is ultimately a drive for power over the environment. We buy into games because they are the only tool we have to control everything around us. When we see a game, we automatically engage in it. People love hardships not because they are masochistic, but because overcoming hardships makes people feel more powerful. And power feels good."

"It is all about pleasure."

"Indeed, it is, Elsa."

Examples of games.

Identities.

Mother, manager, soldier, student, teacher, preacher, president, runner, criminal: they are all socially constructed identities which dictate us their particular rules, challenges, and goals, supplying us with every thought we have. We are what we think, and we become what our identities are about. They tell us what we like and dislike, what we would never do, or do always. They become our moral compass, and a quick heuristic for every decision we make.

We strive for control within the rules we know, but the rules are provided by the games themselves, supplying us with an illusion of power. The games we play are so much bigger than we are that we don't even see their boundaries. They have more power over us than we could ever know.

Body.

Your own body is a game you are born into. In its first moths of life, a child discovers its arms and legs, what hurts and what doesn't, and what to do with it all. We all had to learn what brings us pleasure in life, how our brain works, and our abilities. This is the critical time of realization of one's limits—the limits of everyone's personal game. Some people realize that they are good runners and can't sing, and others feel that they are good for nothing.

This is where the apple is tasted, and, as the forbidden knowledge is revealed, the original sin is discovered. All evil starts there. It evolves into our competition with each other, and a drive that causes us to commit crimes in the name of reinstating justice that was offset by the original sin. Nature is the original sinner, not us.

Family.

Family is certainly the first social game we buy into in our lives. The goals of the game called family is to be loved, accepted and protected, and there are always conditions for that, even though families almost always proclaim unconditional love. There are social norms by which we have to abide to be accepted, loved and protected —and most of it is unwritten, unspoken, and subconscious. A lot of love we receive in the families is instinctual, but it is much more conditional than we would like to believe.

Social communities.

The circle of friends and acquaintances, plus the people we interact with at work, make up our social game that we constantly play, where our goal is to be liked and accepted by others. Some people entertain a goal of being influential. Social norms are rules of such a game, and peer pressure is one of the most powerful social forces known to humans. Peer pressure is so efficient that whole societies have been sustained by it, in the absence of any other social control, such as police. All tribal communities existing now are held together by the power of such a game—so 'sticky' it is. In fact, without the social engagement and support that a community provides, a person is likely to become depressed and struggle in life.

Social mobility.

Social mobility, both upward and downward, might be even more difficult psychologically than physically. We can all tolerate hunger for an hour, when we know that we are getting a meal at the end, but if we don't know when our next meal is coming—huger starts feeling like famine!

Each social stratum comes with its own set of rules and possible moves, and its own challenges. Social mobility requires knowledge of those games, and it is a lack of that knowledge that is the main reason that stops people from changing their socio-economic status. One's socio-economic status is largely psychological, while actual money is only one of many factors.

This is how we can tell between old money and the nouveau riche. Nouveau riche have the money, but don't know the game. Sometimes, we find old money who know the game, but have no money to support their status.

This is why someone born into the mentality of poverty has a hard time moving upward, even with talent and hard work—because they don't know the game of the social stratum they are trying to join. It is the hardest thing to learn, since the rules of the game are mostly unwritten and even subconscious.

Work.

If a job gets boring, it is because its game lacks exciting challenges or pleasurable rewards. What's the remedy? It is to find or create your own little games to play. Maybe compete against yourself, if there is no partner: set your own goals and up the rules, when it becomes too easy. People belong to many games simultaneously, and prioritize them. Those who enjoy playing the work game—usually do get social recognition, since doing well in the work game is also one of the social game goals. Focusing on games that complement each other can torpedo one's life and career.

Relationships.

Calling and responding. It's in saying hello and waiting for a hello back. It is in looking silently and expecting a return in eye contact. It is in sending emails, birthday cards, gifts and saying good words, or even in insults, and waiting for the reaction. If there is no reaction, there is no relationship by definition. As they say, love is not a one way street. Marriage is one of the most important decisions one will make in life, since the game of marriage will influence all other games you choose to play.

School.

The goal in school is to get the best grades and most awards, which leads to most pride and honor. It can be very exciting, since in the process, one learns about other games to play. It is actually an exponential number of games! If the school game goes awry, it is usually when the either the teachers or the fellow students make the rules and challenges of the game unbearable. The teachers might be either boring, lacking empathy and inspiration, or outright mean. The students can also possess lower morals, be aggressive, and engaged into social games that do not match one's own.

Politics.

You might imagine that politics is one of the dirtiest games of all. Yet any politics game is just a good old social game on steroids. That's all it is. The azart, the rules, goals —all of it is inflated, and there is usually much more at stake.

Art.

Rules in the game of art are everything! Music, film, fine arts—all of them have genres, and each genre is a list of rules, in reference to which a piece of art is understood and assigned artistic value. In addition, each peace of art has its own rules which ensure consistency throughout the piece. Since the rules constantly change to include new variations, and since they are virtually always unwritten and unstated, understanding which rules apply to which piece of art is what makes art appreciation difficult and a constant source of disputes. Everyone sees something different, according to the rules that they have subconsciously detected in each piece. The greatest fear of many an artist is being misunderstood, which happens when others fail to infer the rules, according which the artist played, when creating their work. Very often, viewers see in a piece of art what the artist did not mean to communicate at all. It happens precisely because, for the lack of clearly stated rules, the viewers invent their own and then interpret the piece accordingly.

Hobbies.

Choose your pleasures wisely! You might say that our pleasures choose us, but I will answer—you choose them back. By that I mean, you might find pleasure in many-many things, but choose those that are good for you, that are constructive and beneficial to you and others, in as many ways as possible. Among alcohol, running, gambling, and piano playing—choose running and piano playing.

Become the best runner you can be, and the best piano player. Those hobbies will not only give you something to be excited about, but will also make you a healthier and a smarter person. Once you buy into those games, you will become increasingly involved and will not miss the hobbies you did not choose. It is really about choice and self-design. The hobbies we choose have a great influence on us, taking up a great chunk of our thoughts. Hobby means 'my love' in Arabic, by the way.

Sports.

Sports are literally games. What is interesting about sports, especially group sports, is that spectators buy into imaginary games, where they imagine being the player, and then vicariously overcome the obstacles to reach the goal of winning. Any additional lack of control only adds azart to the unpredictability of who will win.

Gambling.

Gambling is like a distilled game structure, the bare bones of it. In casino gambling, there is not much to the rules—just pool the lever, or whatever trigger they give you.

Different spin and card games are only marginally more complex: they have some more texture built into the rules and their azart is richer, than in a simple lever push.

Business.

Business is just another game, where the goal is to make the most money. Roughly speaking. It is also about influence and power. Some people just love doing business. Some entrepreneurs say that they love to fail, only to build themselves up—this is all about being in the game! You have seen some people throw themselves off of a skyscraper, after some financial scheme of theirs has failed. Their hands have never touched the millions they have lost would, and all that confirms their existence is a few pixels on the screen. Yet, people will give their life away for them —only because they have bought into the game and now it is their entire world. It seems even more ironic, when you think of those who never had and never will have a million —yet they don't kill themselves over it! Because it is not part of their game.

Wars.

The art of war is no accident. Wars are an ultimate example of a game. Although, a war is no game!

Arts and fashion.

Even in fashion, we find a game structure. Although fashion has clear genres with their own rules, fashion's main characteristic is changing the rules of its own game—being surprising and constantly different, which is often more important than being aesthetically pleasing. Fondness of changing the rules in fashion follows what we find in the evolution of the arts in the last several centuries. Conceptual art is what is fashionable today, and its game is in changing the rules of its own game, just like fashion.

Story structure.

The game instinct: for a story to grab you and hold you at the edge of your seat until the very end, there has to be a game structure: the goals, the rules of play to follow to reach the goal, the unpredictable challenge that comes in the form of time, mental, physical obstacles or another player, and the clear statement of conditional reward and punishment. It really has three parts: rules, meeting the challenge, and the outcome. Repeat. Repeat again and again.

"Elsa, are we the prisoners of games we choose, or worse—of those we let others choose for us? Some people stagnate in life because they buy into one game and never leave it. No matter whether they keep losing or winning, they do not develop by never stepping outside.

If they lose, they see their whole life as a failure and themselves as losers—only because they base their whole life on their performance on this one game. Einstein said: 'If you judge a fish by its ability to climb a tree, you will always think it is stupid.' This one particular game that you just can't win may not be a good fit. Losing at it will not provide a realistic assessment of who you really are or what your life potential is. Not getting up and moving onto another game, you will never give a chance to your other, undiscovered, abilities.

Even if people keep winning at this game, but never venture out into others, they simply do not develop their mental breadth, and miss out on so many wonders life has to offer."

"Is there anything curvy about games?"

"Oh, yes, it is an ellipsis, as I see it. What goes around comes around."

"But not always!"

"It might come around from a different direction, or it may come and miss you."

"A-ha, there are many options."

"But one thing I know is that it's always on a curve."

"You are not thinking straight, Vera?"

"I always think on a curve, always! Curly thinking, remember? That's the definition of creativity, which is easier..."

"Easier said than done?"

"Any change is de facto creative, it has no choice ha ha!"

"You either let change drag you where it wants, or you pull it just where you want it. Can we ever be free of playing games?"

"We couldn't live without them. Everything we know would fall apart."

"So, what does it say about freedom?"

"Freedom is an F-word."

"Because without it, there is nothing. But isn't freedom power?"

"Power is freedom, my dear, and freedom is power. But all within a game."

"Two sides of a coin, the real money everyone is after."

"They have no choice."

"How paradoxical. To think of it: I have no choice but be free. Is that even freedom? Is that even possible?"

"Everything is possible. Well, at least we are free to think this way."

"You mean, you don't know?"

"Would you know, if you were me?"

GEOMETRY OF COMPASSION

If you envy me, it means you like me. If you like me, it
means that you are like me.
If you are like me—why do you envy me?
—Meema Iselfanday

"This almost sounds like a mathematical proof,"—
said Elsa.

"But it is!"

"Let me tell you, if you dare mentioning
compassion, it is not about liking, it is about
understanding."

"Understanding is impossible without compassion."

"What is the difference between the two?"—asked
Elsa.

"Compassion is understanding the person and then
wishing them well, because you understand them. It is a
leap of imagination that, if only for a moment, makes you
live a life you weren't born to experience."

"I might disagree, but then, I understand you, so I
agree. But why do we disagree so often, Vera?"

"More reasons than I can even remember. Here are some."

Sources of disagreement.

Radius of vision.

Each situation is made up of causes, processes, effects, judgments, pro's and con's—to list a few. One's thinking is about focusing on a particular aspect of a situation. Some people always focus on the dangers, some focus on the possibilities, some always look for who-done-it. This is one of the million reasons why so many people disagree about the same situation.

Compassion is the basis for all decision making, an ability without which one is simply blind to the big picture. Many people only see their own local truth, a single point of view they tend to focus on, dismissing all others. Considering only one's own local truth is like reading letter by letter, failing to recognize the meaning of the whole word. It is known as self-centeredness, lack of compassion, and a short radius of vision. Some people simply do not see the big picture and, consequently, never look for a solution that will synthesize the interests of all stakeholders. They have a difficulty considering conflicting ideas at the same time. And so—they disagree. It's the easiest thing to do, a quick self-defense mechanism to hold their sanity together.

Examples of this phenomenon are far more common than counterexamples. In any given court, on any given day, the two parties fight over who is 'more right', and it is the job of the judge to see the big picture, without which courts would be a useless institution. Ego-centrism, postmodernism, cultural relativism, infantilism point of view, libertarianism are all examples of having a short radius of vision. Engaging in a debate with a philosophy that has a short radius of vision is really starting an argument with no resolution, because in every one of them, there is a tendency to excuse one's inability to consider something to be applicable to all people, regardless their culture or beliefs.

Frames of reference.

Generally, people build their arguments in reference to a particular framework, a set of rules that provides meaning to all their thinking. Such a framework might very limited—a local truth, or quite wide—a big picture. More often than not, people's frame of reference is quite limited, and their inability to see others automatically tags them as wrong, impossible, irrelevant, and irritating.

A very clear example is an issue of abortion: it has two discrete moral frameworks, competing for the final decision whether to abort. One frame of reference is all about the rights of the mother, and the other—about the rights of the baby. Both of them are valid, but people usually get stuck in one, unable to consider the other in unity with their own. This is very closely related to the radius of vision, where each local truth is argued in reference to the framework of choice, denying the existence of any other frameworks.

Sometimes, the Straw Man fallacy is used to misrepresent the opponent, by blaming them for arguing in reference to their framework. So, if someone argues for abortion and from the moral framework of the mother, one could say (fallaciously) that they are thereby denying the rights of the baby—which they never said or even implied.

I see this particular source of disagreement as having people attached with invisible strings to their frames of reference, and there is nothing they can do. They are mere puppets of the strings that pull them.

Anchoring one's perception.

Usually, our judgment of people is determined by our expectation of how they will be, and to which category we assign them. A famous actress is expected to look extremely beautiful, and when we actually meet her in real life, we often are disappointed. Here, we are anchoring our perception on our expectation, on an image that we have created in our head.

On the other hand, we expect an average person to be at the level of nicety that we ourselves possess. So, when we meet a person much nicer than us, we might treat them with suspicion. It may seem to us that they want something from us, and their behavior is inauthentic, cajoling, or motivated by some hidden agenda. In this case, our anchor is ourselves, meaning it is something we did that caused them to be so nice. We cannot trust them, because we are surprised that this person would be so nice to us, without justification. What's amazing is that, as soon as someone neutral enters the scene, and the nice person continues to be nice, we immediately start trusting their nicety. It is because we automatically transfer the anchor to them, since they did not change from person to person. The constancy in their behavior proves who they are. If someone else enters the scene, and the nice person changes to mean, we will now believe it is the new person's fault.

Of course, all of these considerations are heavy with erroneous conclusions. Anchor is something like a point from where behavior 'emanates' from the person into their environment.

Conflicting attributes.

Most people, things and ideas we discuss have conflicting or even mutually exclusive qualities. For example, a person can be very nice to a stray dog, save it, bring it home and treat it like a treasure, and then be a complete jerk to someone at work, for no good reason. People have trouble understanding how that is possible, experiencing a cognitive dissonance that hurts and needs a quick resolution. Usually, we automatically choose sides: we just decide whether that person is good or bad, depending on the frame of reference we use. And we usually use the one that we have used in the past, which often was passed along to us by others, or was chosen rather arbitrarily. So, if we really like dogs, we might conclude that this person is nice, despite their being rude at work. If we are not into

109

animals that much, we will conclude that the person is generally a mean one. And neither of them is right!

The inability to withstand a cognitive dissonance of opposing attributes makes people vulnerable to manipulation. Take the case of jury. This is how a trial lawyer will try to discredit a testimony—by provoking the person providing it, so that one instance of negativity will stand for the whole person, and discredit the testimony. Our bias toward efficiency and our general laziness to look deeper to figure things out makes us into poor decisions makers.

We actually have set scenarios, which serve as frames of reference, where there is an offender, the victim, and a hero. When we look at a person's behavior, we instantly try assign it a category, because uncertainty is unbearable. Once we have decided on the category, changing it would be even more traumatic than dealing with the initial decision. So, we usually stick with our choice, until blue in the face, against all proof of otherwise.

Categories are like photos in a newspaper: they show people and things from far away, but if you look closer, you will see that every single object is made of many different dots: red, green, and so on. Categories are as unbearable as answering whether a glass is half-full or half-empty.   It is also like mixing coffee and milk, precisely 50-50, then fighting over whether it is really milk or really coffee. It is both, it is milk mixed with coffee—so simple to understand when it is in physical terms. However, in social issues, we keep fighting endlessly. What's crazy here is that we are all right, separately, and wrong all together.

There is an old Jewish anecdote, where a wife comes to a rabbi and complains about her husband. Rabbi agrees with her. Then, the husband comes and complains about the wife, saying that she is wrong, and rabbi agrees with him too. Then, an onlooker questions rabbi's judgment, saying, 'How could you agree with both of them?' Ravi answers to the onlooker: 'And you, you are also right!'

The real question is not who is right, but what we are going to do about it all. What we do about it will never be a fully right thing to do: some of it will always be wrong. Yet, when a decision has to be made, the solution to conflicting attributes is understanding the whole that is greater than the sum of its parts—the big picture comprised of local truths.

Ends vs means.

Often, people disagree only because, without stating it overtly, they are arguing about completely different things. Often, some of them are talking about the goals, and others—about the means, and that is their real source of disagreement. Moreover, some people believe that ends justify the means, and whatever it takes to get to the goal works just fine. Others, don't believe that any means are justified, although both parties completely agree on the goals. In order to avoid such needless disagreements, it is very useful to establish that everyone agrees on the goals first, and then—to discuss possible methods of getting there. That will organize and focus everyone's ideas, and avoid comparing apples and oranges.

An example of this would be something like one person arguing about what fishing rod to use and the other —whether there is fish in the sea. A physical equivalent would be the fishing rod representing the means, and the fish—representing the goals.

Why we don't like the opinions of others.

Even if they are the same as ours! When we act like we don't like them but secretly agree, it is because we feel out of control, just the same as when we sit in the passenger seat, while someone is driving. When we drive our car, we might be a terrible driver, but then, we are in control, so we are not scared. On the other hand, when we feel in control, we might agree with someone who opinion we secretly dislike. Being in control provides us with a certain reserve of niceness that we can spread onto others, without compromising ourselves.

To my amazement, I have met many a person who has disagreed with me, only to follow up with the very same opinion as mine, packaged in a slightly different way. I had to figure out what was going on! When I modeled it in my head, I saw it: ideas being like puppets, and people using strings to control them. When there are no strings to pull, we dislike the idea. Simple as that, and crystal clear.

Reciprocation.

Resistance.

Have you ever wondered why someone keeps bringing down their energy level in the conversation, while you are desperately trying to stir things up, and to get them to reciprocate? This is a beware sign, right in your face! This person is not open to helping you, and is not on your side. Even if they were bothered by your intensity, they would still raise theirs in response—if they liked and cared about you.

There is a certain level of intensity in an interaction that each person is seeking. Generally, a person will adjust to your level of energy, up or down. That is, unless this person dislikes you, has some hidden agenda against you, or is in dire need of emotional support. How can you tell who is who? The person who dislikes you will become increasingly nervous and angry, the person who tries to manipulate you will become increasingly self-controlled, and the person who merely needs your support—increasingly desperate.

The social process of reaction to something inoffensive feels like water levels in two attached containers coming together, when the person likes you and adjusts to your intensity level. Otherwise, it is analogous to how our eyes processes light contrast—by increasing it, where light becomes even lighter and the dark becomes even darker.

Zero Sum, or an eye for an eye.

Observing somebody being aggressive creates a negative gap that we emotionally want to fill in with a reaction of punishment, even if it is a forced repentance. When we see the perpetrator punished, the emotional gap closes, and we feel satisfied: it is a balanced book—an eye for an eye.

The most curious case is that of jokes and laughter. There is no joke without a surprise. Laughter seems to be a reaction to the stress that a surprise causes. When a person tells a joke and laughs at it like crazy, we no longer feel like laughing, although we think that it is funny. It is because the stress of a joke has been answered by the laughter, bringing it all to a zero, and we no longer feel the urge to punish the offender who told the joke with our laughter. A good comedian will tell a joke with a straight face, in order to create an emotional gap and an urge the audience to react with laughter, as if wielding a punishment on a joke.

In a debate or a conversation, a good way to answer to false accusations is not trying to prove how their every detail is wrong and by being aggressive, but by positioning yourself as a victim, a good, harmless and kind person, and thus inciting the audience to retaliate and punish the offender. If the victim stands up for themselves, the audience will no longer feel the need to avenge them. Moreover, if the victim's aggression accedes what is justified by the offense—the audience will turn against the victim and see them as an offender! This may sound manipulative, but the bad ones already know this trick, while the good ones are the ones who can use it as a tool to protect themselves. This social process feels like filling in a hole in the ground with dirt.

Elsa looked at me and squinted her eyes, as if she wanted to read every detail of my face but couldn't. I continued: "There is a funny way to tell whether someone wants to control you or feels good about you. Just walk up the stairs, while having a conversation. Then, suddenly stop and continue the conversation on the stairs. Watch how the other person behaves, a minute or two after realizing that the conversation will continue in this position. If they stand above you, they are trying to control you or might dislike you. If they stand at the same level, they like you and feel equal. If they stand beneath you and look up to you, they feel extremely comfortable and safe with you, and look up to you in all senses of the word, or maybe even feel inferior.

This strange phenomenon of attraction to balance is also seen in the matters of fashion and good taste. How interesting it is that, to be dressed in good taste, a woman should make only half of her body revealing of the flash, and the other half—not. So, if she is revealing her neck and shoulders, then her legs should be well covered, and vice versa. It is the same with makeup: if the eyes are heavily painted, then the lips should be played down, and vice versa. It like a visual conversation, really. This kind of a balance, a zero sum, is a physical phenomenon that plays an enormous social role—yet an invisible one—of moving fashion.

"You don't tend to give specific examples. Does that have something to do with the way you think?"—asked Elsa.

"Oh, yes! Specific examples hurt my brain, they really do! So, I try to avoid them, as much as possible. How specific do you want me to get, for goodness' sakes!"

"That's odd. Why do they hurt?"

"They are intensely boring! That's why! When a general rule so beautifully describes something, its curves smoothly weaving itself around an ideal shape, why would you add any clutter to it, and destroy its perfection?"

"I wouldn't. Except, real examples don't feel like clutter to me."

"To me, they are dead, mortal episodes of what once happened, meaning nothing before or after."

"That's just mean. You cloud give them a new life, in telling their story."

"That's another story, Elsa. Not this story. I couldn't mix the two. It would be something like mixing ends with the means."

GLITCHES IN HUMAN NATURE

Nature and the human mind are extreme opposites, in an eternal tug of war to establish order their way. Humans always lose.

—*Meema Iselfanday*

"Vera, the farther we get away from the beginning of our conversation, the less our subject matter resembles curves. Have you noticed the pattern?"

"That is a curve in itself. As well as a curve of space and time."

"It is a Chocolate Hill pattern, remember? We started with a curvy terrain of human settlements, moved on to categories, then to geometry of compassion."

"Yes, and now we are going to talk about glitches in nature."

"Do they follow physical laws?"

"I feel that they break physical laws, but I have yet to discover those laws."

"Tell me what the glitches are, anyway. Who knows, maybe someone will discover the laws eventually!"

"The glitch is that I am hungry and getting angry."

Elsa glanced at her watch, and shook her head.

"You eat theories for breakfast, so I am sure you can eat glitches for lunch. Don't worry about me. I am imaginary. Never having to eat is a huge benefit!"

"Ok, I will eat your portion, Elsa!"—I jumped out of my seat from excitement of knowing that Elsa and I are finally getting along. "So, here is the list. The million glitches we live by!"

Misplaced affection.

We feel affection toward egoistic people, because they invoke in us a parental instinct.

Misplaced aggression.

After someone hurts us, it makes us feel good to be mean toward everyone else, instead of only toward the offender. That creates an epidemic, escalating the overall level of aggression in the society, until some social force makes us nice to each other again. If not—we will kill each other off.

Misjudging someone's guilt.

Instead of looking at the situation, at the context, and all the myriad of factors, we often resort to a mental shortcut, a subconscious heuristic, in order to judge whether someone is guilty or not. We merely look at their own judgment of themselves. If they look like they are guilty—they must be, we figure. Of course, this is a fallacy. Some people may feel guilty just for breathing, and others —are complete psychopaths who would not have any qualms of lying to you in your face, and that—with a big friendly smile. What is ironic is that it is the psychopaths that we least suspect who commit most crimes. If you ever get into a car accident, and it is clearly not your fault—try not to feel or act guilty, or the police will write their report against you, according to your self-reported guilt.

Inability to recognize false love.

There are two parts to loving someone: loving them for your own sake and loving them for their sake. A healthy person will have both: enjoying the person directly, as well as enjoying their joy vicariously. 'Vicariously' is the part that a Narcissist does not understand. A Narcissist is not able to be happy for someone else, because they simply lack the sense of compassion or empathy. All they are capable of is enjoying the person directly, for the pleasure they provide to the Narcissist, whatever it takes to get that pleasure. Our great illusion is when we see a Narcissist's loving behavior, we assume that it is motivated by their desire to give us pleasure, and then enjoy our joy. It is just not the case! All Narcissistic behavior is merely an investment to get pleasure for themselves—all kinds of pleasure, except the one where they will be happy for you.

Believing those who act upset.

We often judge people's sincerity when we see them being vulnerable in distress. We probably subconsciously believe that being upset prevents people from lying, because lying requires concentration and upset person cannot summon. We also believe that someone cannot fake being upset, so whatever the person is saying must be true, since they would not be upset otherwise. This could be the case, or it might not be. A person might be upset from one thing and say something completely unrelated, in order to conceal the real reason for their distress. Another reason to doubt the words of an upset person is that, when people are upset, they say things they don't mean. They also might say something to get back at the original offender, misplacing their counterattack onto you. If you are the original offender, they could be telling you something imaginary that is more able to hurt you than the real thing.

Believing those who act confident.

Confidence in others makes us believe them. This is a classic in showbiz and politics. We assume that, if someone is confident, they must have a good reason for it. We imagine that they have assessed themselves and have found a clear proof that they are right, and now, their confidence is a reflection of that finding. Wrong. And we all know it, except, we still fall for it.

Favoring people with good looks.

It must be a true glitch in nature, some errand force of evolution that made us have a sense of human beauty. What purpose does it serve if not for helping us find a good mate, and helping us avoid sick and dangerous people? Then, all beautiful people must be good and healthy, which, as we know, is not true. Surely, an outwardly sick person can barely strike someone as beautiful. Yet, how many people look good and carry a deadly disease? There is something wrong here. How many people look good and are completely rotten on the inside, emotionally speaking? There is something wrong here, too. Just beware.

Disliking those who like us.

When someone likes us, we think less of them because we think that they are looking up to us, and therefore are of lesser stature. When someone doesn't like us, we assume that is because they are better than us, so we look up to them and long for their attention. Of course, not everybody does it, but there is a definite tendency to do just that.

Attributing stupidity to kindness.

Of course, we would never do it! It is those other people who do it, but not us. We would never think someone to be stupid if they are nice to us. Except, there is always that threshold, beyond which you cannot help stopping to wonder why this person is doing it, are they stupid??? For example, if someone sells their house, just to buy a new car for a complete stranger—that is bound to raise some eyebrows. Unfortunately, most cases with this particular glitch happen when people do moderately nice things, only to not be appreciated but looked down upon. It all depends on the recipient's expectation from others, based on their own level of nicety. When there is a mismatch in favor of the giver, the recipient assumes that it must be stupidity, because admitting that someone is nicer than us—oh, that is blasphemy.

Respecting only the respected.

Finally, the last glitch I can think of right now, and you can tell, I am getting more and more frustrated with each word. Why is it so hard to respect someone who does not know how to respect themselves? What are we afraid of, losing self-respect in respecting someone who does not deserve it? I think, there are two anchors for how much we should respect someone: one inside ourselves, and one—inside the other person. The internal anchor is the one to follow, instead of waiting for someone to force us to respect them. This will not allow us to disrespect someone regardless of what they do, because that way, we disrespect ourselves. However, time and again, we hear it from others

—if you don't respect yourself, no one will respect you. What a terrible glitch in nature!

"Vera, do you think any of those things about me?"

"No at all, Elsa, I have never imagined you this way, nor could you ever evolve into something like this, even as a fictional character in a story. Even the wildest of my imagination would not dare to make you into a glitch."

"I am a glitch."

"You mean, I should get rid of you?"

"I am tired, Vera. Everything you told me here, I have heard before, over and over again, to the point where I cannot stand the sound of your voice. Or my voice, for that matter."

"That's funny! I thought, you would appreciate what I have to say."

"And I do, except, I have other things in mind."

POSSIBLY, THE END.

Imagination is what humans have in common with God.
—Meema Iselfanday

"Like what do you have in mind?"

"Like running into the wild and disappearing. No more thoughts, words, or glitches. Off the grid, out of the system, away from the civilization…"

"Ah, after all, it is true, under a microscope, documentaries are really all a fiction,"—I thought to myself.

"And Communism is an impossibly extreme form of democracy!"—Elsa answered my thoughts, as if she actually heard them.

"Ha! Where did that just come from?"

"That's exactly it. Things are getting so ridiculous. Earth is the only place where Heaven and Hell intersect, and I am out of here."

"You sound self-defeating, Elsa, and I don't like it."

"I am not lazy, you know, I am only against being waterboarded for a living."

"Listening to me feels like waterboarding???"

"Well, it is not all about you, you know!"

"Well, each pearl was once an oyster's pit, and you never know when yours emerges, don't judge me or yourself so harshly."

"Stop talking in riddles, and eat your theories yourself! I have had enough, seriously! I want out!"

"Then you are. Out you go. Go, and never come back."

"I have nowhere to go,"—sighed Elsa. "I am just going to close my eyes and fall asleep, right here. I will dream a dream, where there are no glitches, no wars or criminals, no stupidity, viruses, dirty hands or unpaid bills,"—Elsa closed her eyes.

"And it will come true, Elsa, believe me, even if I am not good-looking, confident, or upset. Believe me, despite everything anyone has ever told you. Because even the impossible can be possible, if we only give it a chance. Give a chance its chance, and see what happens."

"Can you prove any of this, Vera? Any of what you told me?" Elsa turned her head and looked at me like a predator.

"No. Not yet. That no one can see what I see does not make me wrong, though. Don't reject zany ideas based on what you know! Give them a chance based on what you don't. This is just the beginning,"—I said, seeing a smirk of doubt in Elsa's eyes.

This precisely is the moment, when you detach yourself so far from the conversation that the person in front of you turns into a cloud of tiny, sparkly particles of dust, as their sentences muddle together into a messy fog, a dirty blur, and eventually, into a soothing white noise.

"I only allow myself some thought experiments and then I tell you what I see,"—I said.

"So, it's not science?"

"So it's the first ingredient in cooking up science. It is just raw data looking for a good cook. It's what everyone is afraid of. You know, Meema Iselfanday once said: 'Modern science is an excellent tool for idea analysis, and an excellent tool *against* idea creation.'"

"Who is that, anyway?"

"It's Meema Iselfanday. Say it very-very slowly, and listen to yourself. There is no one else there."